THE INNOVATOR'S DISCUSSION

Few ideas about innovation and entrepreneurship have caught on as well as the lean-startup approach. However, despite incorporating this technique into their work, most innovative entrepreneurial teams still fail. This book tells you why – and shows you how to develop the conversational skills that differentiate successful teams from the rest.

Based on 6 years of detailed empirical analysis of teams at the forefront of technological breakthroughs and new venture creation, *The Innovator's Discussion* shows you how high-performance teams verbally accomplish their work. Through engaging examples, exercises, and descriptions, it enables entrepreneurs to develop the conversational competencies that can help them create new products and ventures.

The book includes a technique for making interpretation visible that enables teams to navigate pivots in the innovation process. It also includes the materials and instructions for the *Toasted Marshmallow* game designed to help entrepreneurial teams fail forward.

The Innovator's Discussion enables readers and their teammates to build a conversational advantage. The reader will gain both a practical and a theoretical understanding of the role of conversation in the context of entrepreneurial work. It is invaluable for aspiring and established entrepreneurs as well as for educators and those wanting to learn more about entrepreneurship, innovation, and high-performance teams.

Betsy Campbell, PhD, researches the practices of teams at the forefront of science and technology. As a Penn State faculty member, she leads an initiative focused on the democratization of innovative entrepreneurship. Earlier in her career she founded Harvard Alumni Entrepreneurs, Inc. and co-directed the MIT CI Lab.

THE INNOVATOR'S DISCUSSION

The Conversational Skills of Entrepreneurial Teams

Betsy Campbell

LONDON AND NEW YORK

First published 2019
by Routledge
2 Park Square, Milton Park, Abingdon, Oxon OX14 4RN

and by Routledge
52 Vanderbilt Avenue, New York, NY 10017

Routledge is an imprint of the Taylor & Francis Group, an informa business

© 2019 Betsy Campbell

British Library Cataloguing-in-Publication Data
A catalogue record for this book is available from the British Library

Library of Congress Cataloging-in-Publication Data
Names: Campbell, Betsy, 1966– author.
Title: The innovator's discussion : the conversational skills of
    entrepreneurial teams / Betsy Campbell.
Description: Abingdon, Oxon ; New York, NY : Routledge, 2019. |
    Includes index.
Identifiers: LCCN 2018053388 | ISBN 9781138497924 (hardback) |
    ISBN 9781138497917 (pbk.) | ISBN 9781351017510 (ebook)
Subjects: LCSH: Creative ability in business. | Teams in the workplace. |
    Communication in management. | New products. | Technological
    innovations—Management. | Entrepreneurship.
Classification: LCC HD53 .C358 2019 | DDC 658.4/022—dc23
LC record available at https://lccn.loc.gov/2018053388

ISBN: 978-1-138-49792-4 (hbk)
ISBN: 978-1-138-49791-7 (pbk)
ISBN: 978-1-351-01751-0 (ebk)

Typeset in Bembo
by Apex CoVantage, LLC

For Glenn and Barbara Campbell
Thank you for all of your help and encouragement.

CONTENTS

ABOUT THE AUTHOR

Dr. Campbell focuses her research on the practices of teams at the forefront of technological innovation and scientific discovery. Earlier in her career Campbell did research at Harvard University and co-directed the Massachusetts Institute of Technology Community Innovation Lab. She also was awarded a Ghiso Fellowship to study at the Yale University Center for Bioethics and was a visiting scholar at the Hastings Center. Campbell was the founder of two high-tech ventures and one nonprofit – Harvard Alumni Entrepreneurs, Inc. – which supports innovators and entrepreneurs around the world. As part of an intrapreneurial business unit, her work helped position an established software company for a $1.5 billion acquisition by Lucent Technologies. Campbell is an active member of the Explorers Club. Previously she served as a subcommittee co-chair for the Harvard Alumni Association Board of Directors. She also has been an invited judge and advisor many times for the MIT Innovation, Development, Enterprise, Action, and Service (IDEAS) socially responsible venture competition. She is the author of *Practice Theory in Action: Empirical Studies of Interaction in Innovation and Entrepreneurship.*

ACKNOWLEDGMENTS

A book about conversational competencies should have its roots in some good conversations. Fortunately I've been part of many productive exchanges with people near and far during the writing process. Similarly, I have benefited from many formative interactions with people long before the idea for the research behind this book began. I am grateful for the many kind and generous conversations that have made this book possible.

I am indebted to the scholars at Massachusetts Institute of Technology and Harvard University, whose rich and relevant research inspired me to conduct research that defied easy categorization. Eric von Hippel and Florence Sender introduced me to the concept of entrepreneurship in their New Enterprise class, a class that changed the direction of my career. The leaders of MIT's Center for Reflective Community Practice of Harvard University's Project Zero deserve a special expression of gratitude. Ceasar McDowell, Joy Amulya, Howard Gardner, David Perkins, and Daniel Wilson all shaped my thinking and showed me how I might investigate my interests. They cared about the ways that theory and practice can intersect, insights that have influenced all my work including the content and style of this book.

The people I know through the University of Exeter also deserve a note of gratitude, especially Adrian Bailey, Andi Smart, John Bessant, and Bill Gartner. Without their support I would not have been able to follow my authentic scholarly interests; I would not have been able to start recording and analyzing the real-time interactions of innovative entrepreneurial teams at work.

Similarly, members of the Penn State University community must be recognized. The College of Education's Krause Innovation Studio and Scott McDonald, in particular, made it possible for me to run workshops and offer courses that refined the games and exercises found in this book.

I am thankful to the community of people who helped in the early days of Harvard Alumni Entrepreneurs, Inc. Jeff Beherens, Tom Black, Steve Herbert, Howard Zaharoff, and many others from this vibrant community have supported and encouraged my interest in entrepreneurial practices and in the creation of experiences for entrepreneurial learning. Those early days also were influenced by Valdur Koha, Arthur Nelson, and Throop Wilder. My interactions with them shaped my thinking about innovative entrepreneurial work, emerging ventures, and the scaffolding needed by aspiring entrepreneurs.

The innovative entrepreneurial teams that permitted me to watch, record, and analyze their team meetings deserve a special thank you. Simply put, their openness made this book possible. Without it, the detailed insights that have been made about the conversational competencies of teams engaged in innovative entrepreneurial work could not have been identified or shared.

My family, too, has played an important role in the work that I do and in the completion of this book. Without them, especially Barbara and Glenn Campbell, I never would have considered a second career that emphasized research and writing. And without their support and encouragement I would not have been able to engage in the time-consuming work that has resulted in this book.

There were also many people who helped me navigate the publishing process. Alistair Croll, Neil Jenkins, and Ellen Reeves provided guidance along the way. And my thoughtful editorial team at Routledge, including Kristina Abbotts, Kate Fornadel, Christiana Mandizha, and many others, helped me bring the project to completion.

Last but by no means least, there are the people who make even the toughest days better; a conversation with these folks about anything can refresh my energy. Among these cherished supporters I include Delane Bredvik, Andrew Carey, Dee Clayton, Tricia Craig, Svend Feddrich, Andrew Groh, Rob Peagler, Caroline Rook, John Schectman, Fumiko Shigeno, Yoichi Takagi, and John White. And then there are Sam and David B. Silberman. A whole book would be required to express all of my gratitude to them. Thank you.

INTRODUCTION

Words, in my not-so-humble opinion, are our most inexhaustible source of magic.
— The character Dumbledore in *Harry Potter*
and the Deathly Hallows Part II (film)[1,2]
Copyright © Warner Brothers, 2011

Words are powerful. While they might not be technically magic, they are the fundamental building blocks of every product and venture ever created. Words give rise to the conversational competencies that enable innovative entrepreneurial teams to do their work. Without thoughtful words and interactions, teams would be hard-pressed to exist let alone to create breakthrough inventions and successful ventures. Simply put, innovative entrepreneurial teams use words to talk their products and ventures into being.[3]

Because the creation of new ventures is never linear, teams must revise their products and plans through conversation as ideas are transformed into realities. The words that enable these conversations serve as a continuously renewable source of possibilities. In each interaction, teams are establishing, maintaining, and evolving what they can do, how they can do it, and who they can become. And even in the most difficult circumstances – those days when your team's time, money, and social capital are all depleted – your words still function at full power. Your words still make it possible for you to build something great out of seemingly nothing.

However, word choices and language forms are not all created equal. Some can help teams craft, revise, and validate ideas more adeptly than others. Fortunately, just as magic incantations can be mastered by aspiring wizards, the conversational competencies associated with innovative entrepreneurial work can be learned by people interested in creating successful ventures. This book can be your guide.

To be clear: This is not a book about pitching or giving presentations. It is not a book about persuasive or charismatic speaking. And it is not a book about marketing communications. This is a book about intra-team conversations. It is about the backstage, day-to-day, mundane conversations you have with your teammates.

This book hones in on the formal and informal team meetings you have almost every day when you are developing a new product, service, or solution. Using examples from lean-startup teams, the concepts presented in the following chapters are especially relevant to high-tech innovative entrepreneurial teams. They also are applicable to teams inventing new products and services in established companies and to teams negotiating new possibilities in response to age-old conflicts in the world. Because the truth is, significant innovation of all kinds is hard, accomplished in teams, and dependent on human interactions – especially face-to-face, verbal conversations.

While the information in this book is meant to be accessible to all, it is not going to dispense commonsense advice about conversations. The book is not going to tell you to speak one at a time in your meetings, for example, even though that is a good tip. Rather, the book is going to give you practical advice derived from studies with high- and low-performance teams about how to improve your team's innovation conversations. **It is going to show you the conversational differences between the master teams and disaster teams, and it is going to present a set of exercises and activities that can help your team improve its conversational competencies.**

Most successful ventures require a team

Although entrepreneurship often is associated with individual visionaries, most successful new ventures are started by teams.[4,5,6,7] The basic definition of a team is a small group of people who are committed to using their skills for a common purpose.[8] However, innovative entrepreneurial teams are a bit more specialized than that. Like cockpit crews, operating room personnel, and military units, innovative entrepreneurial teams tend to be composed of skilled specialists who engage in shared tasks that unfold in unpredictable circumstances within limited time frames. They tend to be what is called "action teams".[9]

Over the past 40 years, research has shown that the intra-team conversations of successful action teams are marked by different language patterns than unsuccessful ones. As a result, training for action teams has been enhanced to include modules on conversational structures – and outcomes have improved in terms of safety and satisfaction. However, even though innovative entrepreneurial teams fit the definition of action teams, they were not part of that body of research.

I had long wondered if there might be a relationship between the way entrepreneurial teams talked and the outcomes for their ventures. In the late 1990s when I was in the earliest stages of starting my second venture, I had an advisor who gave me some advice about language. He told me that when he was in an exploratory mode for a new venture, he phrased everything with the word *might*. He encouraged me to do the same, even in my conversations with potential funders. I was worried that it would make me look uncertain about the venture – and therefore unworthy of investment. He reminded me that I, like every founder, *was* uncertain, and it would be to my advantage to articulate my awareness of that rather than trying to hide the fact.

His words of wisdom stayed with me. When I learned about the language and performance research in other workplaces, I became curious about whether there might be specific conversational markers associated with high-performance innovative entrepreneurial teams. In 2011, I began recording and analyzing the naturally occurring workplace conversations of this type of team in action. The research process is deeply detailed; each conversation is transcribed to include every element – including pauses timed to the second and every utterance of um – and the transcripts are analyzed line by line to reveal the structure of conversation.

This book draws on the findings from those investigations in combination with the knowledge from workplace interaction research more generally. The excerpts and profiles throughout the book represent real innovative entrepreneurial teams. In all cases the names of the people, products, and companies have been changed. In some cases, minor editing and blending have been done for clarity and brevity, and details about their innovations in progress have been obscured.

The book is not based only on scholarly research and academic theory, however; I have firsthand experience participating in the work of innovative entrepreneurial teams. Much earlier in my career I was involved in the founding of several high-tech innovation teams and in the creation of a new business unit inside of an established software company. I also founded Harvard Alumni Entrepreneurs, Inc., a 501(c)(3) that supports entrepreneurs and interdisciplinary innovation efforts around the world. My research interests – and the content of this book – have been influenced greatly by these and other experiences in the entrepreneurial ecosystem.

Why talk about talk

Entrepreneurial work, like all teamwork, is a verbal phenomenon.[10] Interpersonal interaction is essential to the creation and ongoing operations of organizations.[11] And, as David Perkins has asserted, because organizations are conversations, what matters is the *quality* of those conversations.[12]

Talk between teammates is powerful. Intra-team conversations are not neutral exchanges or binary systems of information given and received. They are the means by which thoughts, feelings, values, and beliefs are shared and interpreted. They enhance or inhibit our ability to bond with others, learn new materials, and accomplish shared goals. Simply put, the realities of an entrepreneurial context are created, sustained, and evolved through intra-team conversations. From the moment you first drew an idea on the back of a napkin in a conversation with a trusted colleague you were beginning to talk your venture into being, and you continue to evolve your venture in every team meeting.

Despite the importance of conversation to entrepreneurial work, few teams consciously consider their verbal dynamics. Most native speakers of English tend to think that talk just exists,[13] that it is not worthy of examination, overt reflection, or conscious cultivation. However, their ideas about language in action tend to be very limited.[14] Researchers have shown that social actions are verbally accomplished in ways that defy the expectations of most people. They also have shown that interactional practices (and workplace processes and outcomes) can be improved by focusing on select conversational moves. In other words, by focusing on the way they talk, teams can develop another possible advantage in their quest to succeed. What, then, constitutes a quality conversation?

Positive workplace interactions are situationally accomplished, yet they have shared markers that transcend a specific conversation, topic, or workplace. In general, constructive conversations support sustained discourse and allow for information and insights to be thoughtfully processed aloud. At a more granular level, such conversations tend to incorporate verbal moves that enable collaborative engagement, encourage a flexible stance, and facilitate reflective practice. They are attentive to the contributions and feelings of the people participating. They also are aware of the complexities and uncertainties inherent in the process of doing innovative entrepreneurial work.

Language is rarely front of mind while we are engaged in conversation (unless it is a foreign language). Consequently, people can benefit from exercises that focus attention on language. Structured activities can help teams develop collaborative, provisional, and reflective conversational moves. Similarly, the process of documenting the innovation process can help teams become aware of (and then thoughtfully discuss) aspects of their work that had previously been hidden.

Making your innovation process visible enables you to recognize the different perspectives held by various teammates as well as your resources, assumptions, and options. The documentation of the way your team works can be an ongoing factor in improving your entrepreneurial practice. Doing the documentation process gives your team an opportunity to be reflective and to think expansively. It encourages you to apply both interpretive and analytical lenses to your active work. And it facilitates conversations that are both sensitive to people and responsive to the processes associated with validating products and launching ventures.

Pivots, pivots, everywhere

While the term pivot has been a bit overused in the past 10 years, the concept of pivoting is still relevant to innovative entrepreneurial work. It is worth revisiting the fundamental activities that undergird pivoting.

The path of an innovative entrepreneurial team is never linear. As a team enacts its work it will need to revise its product and strategy numerous times. These changes, of course, depend upon a team being able to notice incongruous factors and to undo (and redo) aspects of its plans and products. Rarely do teams scrap everything and start entirely anew. Rather, teams pivot – they continue to adhere to some existing features of a product and ways of working while they opt to revise others.

To successfully do a pivot, a team must be able to notice and constructively talk about the following:

- Relevant features to retain or change
- Assumptions that have guided their work
- Reasons for past decisions and developments
- Alternative perspectives and explanations

While many books approach pivots as an analytical challenge, this book recognizes that they are also interpretive challenges. What you think you know is always subject to revision based on the acquisition of new information or the reassignment of meanings.

Interpretive language fosters the situated humility, cognitive agility, and creative empiricism necessary for innovative work. Of course, the feeling of being (even falsely) certain is pleasurable. It takes discipline to continually remember that the iterative work of innovative entrepreneurs is framed by plausibility rather than perfection or permanency – and that entrepreneurs always must be ready to revisit and reconsider their assumptions and decisions. Collaborative, provisional, and reflective language can expand your ways of knowing to accommodate the many uncertainties that accompany the accomplishment of innovative entrepreneurial work.

The exercises in this book will build your awareness of the power of interpretive language forms. The exercises will help your team notice flaws in your assumptions and the habitual patterns that guide your work, including your pivoting process. As you incorporate the book's suggested activities into your work, your team will have a new understanding of how to pivot. Whether you are grappling with your first change of direction for your prototype or you are navigating a final change of direction for your company as you approach an acquisition (or a less-celebrated exit), you will be better prepared by mastering the core conversational competencies highlighted in the coming chapters. As your team develops its ability to engage in interpretive conversations, it will undergo a qualitative transformation. Your team will go from knowing *what* to do to knowing *how* to do the iterative process associated with innovation and new venture creation.

Revisiting your motivations

The process of mastering interpretive language can prompt you to think about your motivations for becoming an entrepreneur. For example, according to the Global Entrepreneurship Monitor (GEM), a long-running project that studies entrepreneurship around the world, 69% of U.S.-based entrepreneurs decide to start ventures in order to gain more independence or improve their income.[15] Founders who are driven by a yearning to be in control might not feel comfortable at first with collaborative, reflective, and provisional language, for example. Using these language forms invites different perspectives and multiple voices into team meetings. Consequently, using these conversational moves might make some founders take stock of their core reasons for starting a company.

Research has shown that only very few first-time founders can remain in total control and also generate significant wealth.[16] Instead, founders must decide which motivating factor will guide their actions and their venture. Founders who opt for wealth generally achieve this outcome by accepting a smaller piece of a bigger pie. That means that they are involving other people, especially their teammates, in the fundamental choices and practices related to the company, its product, and its processes. Because language is a primary link between individual participation in a shared activity and the co-creation of a new product or venture, collaborative, reflective, and provisional language can help entrepreneurial teams achieve the necessary agility to work together productively.

Making use of this book

This book highlights several essential ideas. First and foremost, entrepreneurial ventures are conversational accomplishments. Entrepreneurial teams use interpretive language to enact the creation of new products and new companies. These conversational moves include collaborative, provisional, and reflective language forms. Conversational competencies can be learned, and they can be applied to the full array of challenges that face entrepreneurial teams. And finally, the way that your team talks shapes the enduring culture of your company and influences who joins and stays with your team.

The structure of the book has been crafted to familiarize you with the conversational competencies of innovative entrepreneurial teams and to help you develop these skills. The first section is devoted to articulating some popular approaches to innovative entrepreneurial work, including their limitations. The second section explores the three conversational competencies that differentiate high- and low-performance innovative entrepreneurial teams. They are collaborative, provisional, and reflective language forms. You can remember the set as CPR for your venture. The third section offers tips on how you and your team can develop these conversational competencies. It includes a set of exercises to help you develop collaborative, provisional, and reflective conversational moves. It also includes a practice of documentation that can help your team analyze and improve the way that it pivots and operates in general. The fourth section explains how your team can get the most out of these conversational competencies. It touches on several of the inflection points that face founders, including how to talk productively about closing down a venture. The fifth section invites you to participate in a community of practice and hones in on common questions about conversational competencies. One key resource that you will find in the fifth section is a website related to this book – www.innovatorsdiscussion.com – which includes examples, exercises, updates, and insights from the field to help your team ascend. As the book nears its conclusion, you will find an Appendix that gives you the basic materials for the *Toasted Marshmallow* game to help you and your teammates fail forward from an idea that you need to retire or from a venture that you need to shut down. The game pieces in the Appendix also include a special set of cards for teams that are closing a venture because of an acquisition. And finally, the book ends with a short Glossary of key terms.

The activities presented in the third section are designed to be applied to real-world concerns. Some entrepreneurs will want to try them out as independent activities, and others will wait until there is a problem before experimenting with them. Regardless of your entry point into these activities, you will find that you will get the most out of them by making them an ongoing and frequently used part of your entrepreneurial practice.

At first, the exercises and documentation process might seem strange or even unnecessary in an innovative entrepreneurial context. However, I encourage you to see the exercises as a concert pianist sees arpeggios and scales. The pianist knows that the arpeggios and scales build strength, agility, and coordination. These benefits will improve the pianist's ability to perform difficult musical compositions. Similarly, I encourage you to think of the documentation exercise the way a golfer thinks of filming his or her golf swing. By looking at the video, the golfer is able to gain valuable insights about his or her technique that had been undetectable before. Armed with that awareness, the golfer is able to adjust the swing and play a better game. In other words, the exercises and documentation process are essential to your preparation and your improvement as an innovative entrepreneur.

You might notice that there are no worksheets or checklists in this book. While it is a resource for aspiring innovators and entrepreneurs, the book is not a workbook in the classic sense. Instead, the book offers activities that you can incorporate into your regular work. It gives you a framework to help you have productive backstage conversations within your team. In addition to the explicit exercises described in the middle of the book, each chapter concludes with a collection of key ideas and a set of open-ended questions for you to consider with your team from time to time.

The point of doing these activities and building your conversational competencies is to give your current endeavor its best chance of success. Plus, the benefits you get from developing your skills through these exercises will transcend a single venture's performance. With your new verbal abilities, you will be able to make valuable contributions as a member of future teams, as an advisor to other organizations, or as a leader elsewhere in the entrepreneurial ecosystem.

The fundamentals of conversational competencies are beneficial whether you alone are reading this book, if your whole team is reading it, or if you are part of an accelerator that requires the entire cohort to read it. (The fundamentals also apply if you are on a team unrelated to entrepreneurship.) Ultimately, your team should develop its conversational competencies, but a single individual who regularly utilizes these conversational moves within a team can make a significant and positive impact.

Tips for reading this book in different contexts

You might be reading this book as part of your participation in a workshop or course, or you might be reading it on your own. In the first context, the facilitator of your learning group probably will direct your engagement with the readings, the exercises, and the documentation process. The activities in the book are aligned with the practice turn in entrepreneurship education, and they will complement the learning objectives associated with most accelerators.

Many readers, of course, are reading this book on their own or with a cofounder at their own pace. In these circumstances, you can set aside time in a team meeting to experiment with the individual exercises and discuss your experience of them with each other. You also can add the documentation process to your meetings to help you pivot or manage other dilemmas of founding teams. And you can play the *Toasted Marshmallow* game if you find yourself close to an exit for your venture. Building awareness of your conversational habits, competence in your language use, and knowledge of your interpretive processes will give your team additional advantages as you grapple with the many challenges of validating a new product and launching a successful venture.

Talking your venture into being

Learning how to do innovative entrepreneurial work and how to be an innovative entrepreneur is never a simple or straightforward task. And because of the dynamic context of entrepreneurial work, people who opt for entrepreneurial careers are never done honing their abilities. Whether you are just getting started with your first venture or have years of experience as a serial founder, this book will give you one more advantage – conversational competencies – in your quest to build a viable venture and enjoy your entrepreneurial work.

It would be nice if you could just cast a spell and have a validated product and a successful venture materialize out of thin air. However, as powerful as words are, they do not work exactly in that way. Nevertheless, the collaborative, provisional, and reflective language forms described in this book can help your team talk your venture into being. You will find that conversational competencies are an infinite source of innovative entrepreneurial magic, indeed.

Notes

1 Rowling, J. K. (2007). *Harry Potter and the deathly hallows*. New York, NY: Scholastic Press.
2 Yates, D. (Writer). (2011). Harry Potter and the deathly hallows, Part 2. In D. Heyman, D. Barron, & J. K. Rowling (Producer). USA: Warner Bros. Entertainment.

3   Heritage, J. (1984). *Garfinkel and ethnomethodology*. Cambridge: Polity Press.
4   Gartner, W. B., Shaver, K. G., Gatewood, E., & Katz, J. (1994). Finding the entrepreneur in entrepreneurship. *Entrepreneurship: Theory and Practice*, *18*(3), 5–9.
5   Kamm, J. B., Shuman, J. C., Seeger, J. A., & Nurick, A. J. (1990, Summer). Entrepreneurial teams in new venture creation: A research agenda. *Entrepreneurship Theory and Practice*, 7–17.
6   Lechler, T. (2001). Social interaction: A determinant of entrepreneurial team venture success. *Small Business Economics*, *16*(4), 263–278 .
7   Timmons, J. A. (1989). *The entrepreneurial mind*. Andover, MA: Brick House Publishing.
8   Katzenback , J. R., & Smith, D. K. (2005, July–August). The discipline of teams. *Harvard Business Review*, *83*(7), 162.
9   Edmondson, A. C. (2003). Speaking up in the operating room: How team leaders promote learning in interdisciplinary action teams. *Journal of Management Studies*, *40*(6), 1419–1452.
10 Donnellon, A. (1996). *Team talk: The power of language in team dynamics*. Boston, MA: Harvard Business School Press.
11 Cooren, F. (2013). *Interacting and organizing: Analyses of a management meeting*. NJ: Routledge.
12 Perkins, D. N. (2003). *King Arthur's round table: How collaborative conversations create smart organizations*. Wiley.
13 Schegloff, E. A. (1996). Confirming allusions: Toward an empirical account of action. *American Journal of Sociology*, *102*(1), 161–216.
14 Speer, S. (2005). The interactional organization of the gender attribution process. *Sociology*, *39*(1), 67–87.
15 Kelley, D., Ali, A., Brush, C., Corbett, A., Daniels, C., Kim, P., Rogoff, E. (2016). Global entrepreneurship monitor: 2015. United States Report: Babson College and Baruch College.
16 Wasserman, N. (2012). *The founder's dilemmas: Anticipating and avoiding the pitfalls that can sink a startup*. Princeton, NJ: Princeton University Press.

PART 1

Defining the problem

Cultural norms about what it means to be an innovator or an entrepreneur are always present. American culture has put high-tech, high-growth entrepreneurs, in particular, on a pedestal. These expectations can influence the behavior of aspiring entrepreneurs, sometimes to their detriment. The following section unpacks some of the popular myths about entrepreneurs. It describes the ways that these myths can undermine the effectiveness of entrepreneurial innovation teams in action.

1

MISPERCEPTIONS THAT PREVENT TEAMS FROM INNOVATING SUCCESSFULLY

From teams of experts to expert teams

No doubt, creating new ventures and innovating new products and services is difficult. Challenges can come from many sources: access to resources, awareness of the market, and technical ability to develop the product are just a few. Challenges also come from (or can be exacerbated by) the ways that team members interact with each other.

Perhaps the idea that the verbal behaviors within teams can be a significant problem comes as a surprise. When teams – especially entrepreneurial innovation teams – are being formed a lot of attention is given to the characteristics of the members, and the following questions are often asked:

- Do the members have complementary skills that will enable them to build and sell a product or service?
- Does each person have competence in his/her area of expertise as evidenced by educational and professional experiences?
- Have the team members worked successfully together before?

These traits might confer advantages on the teams that possess them. However, all too often, these guidelines produce teams of experts rather than expert teams. How team members interact turns out to be just as important as who the team members are.

In other words, advantages can come from a team's conversational competencies as well as from its composition. In fact, the presence (or absence) of certain conversational markers can identify teams that are likely to achieve high and low levels of success even before they complete version 1.0 of a product.

To explain better what is meant by conversational competencies, let's examine a description of a workplace interaction of an early-stage, high-tech innovation team. Just months into their project, Andy and his co-founders are deep into developing a product prototype. They even are getting reactions to it from prospective customers. They are doing their best to follow the lean startup method for entrepreneurial success. Here is a description of one of their team meetings:

> Andy, the leader of the UhOhCo founding team, says that he is confident that their emerging product is "better than anything else out there" and lists several features that are currently functioning or almost done. Bridgette says to Andy, "I agree with you 100% about the technology. But we're not so good with ease of use – at least that's what we've been hearing." She then turns her attention to Carol and continues: "And I think that is what you were referring to but I may be wrong." Carol confirms that Bridgette has understood her concerns. Andy instantly minimizes the critique: "But ease of use is just a kind of an issue for people getting started. They have to upload some information, and the way it is is the best way to design it . . ." He continues, "You know, there's this paradigm and I want – this needs to be in our heads – consumer producers." Carol shows that she remembers that conversation from a few days back by making the "mmhm" sound. Andy reinforces his point: "Okay? And ultimately that's what I want to create, a customer base of consumer producers."

This team could be on the verge of what some might call a pivot-or-persevere meeting. Bridgette and Carol seem inclined to look for product pivots – changes that could be made to their emerging product to make it more commercially viable. Andy is of a different mind. He wants to continue to execute the existing plan and develop the prototype that they had originally envisioned. However, the team does not consciously change directions or stay the course in this meeting. They actually churn in place for 6 more weeks. Week after week they repeat this conversation more or less, until they disband without completing any product at all.

The challenges facing UhOhCo, at least at this moment, are not based on technical abilities, limited resources, or market information. In fact, this team has just received some money and in-kind resources and, as indicated in the excerpt, have an abundance of market feedback. Moreover, the team is comprised of top-notch engineers and business people who have the necessary know-how to build products and ventures. Instead, this team is challenged by the task of interpretation. They are struggling to make sense of the customer feedback in a way that can productively shape their emerging product and young venture.

Managing interpretive tasks is a large part of what innovation teams must do, and most meaning-making occurs through in-person conversations. Given that everyone has a basic capacity for verbal exchange, one could easily assume that meaning-making through conversation would be a simple affair. But one would be wrong. Ascribing meaning can take several forms: knowing what someone else means and intends, relating experiences to actions and next steps, and connecting events to external ideals and obligations, for example.[1]

With these ideas about meaning-making in mind let's look again at UhOhCo's conversation. They do not seem to be struggling with the intersubjective tasks of making sense of fellow team members. They comprehend each other's points, and when Bridgette is not sure if she has understood Carol's point, she is comfortable asking about it. They do seem to have difficulties with the actional tasks of meaning-making. Rather than finding ways that disruptive feedback from customers could impact their prototype, the team dismisses the feedback and clings to the original vision, for example. One explanation for this inflexible reaction might come from the team's desire to adhere to external models of what it means to *be* an entrepreneur.

Being entrepreneurial

Entrepreneurs in American culture have high status. Pop culture associates them with attractive qualities such as bravery, ambition, self-sufficiency, and the ability to lead change.[2,3] American ideals such as individualism, industriousness, and inventiveness are attributed to them. In short, they are regarded as contemporary hero figures. They are sometimes treated as celebrities, and celebrities increasingly are becoming entrepreneurs.

Entrepreneurs and aspiring entrepreneurs are surrounded by these normative concepts. Magazine covers, mainstream movies, popular books, and the nightly news all feature entrepreneurs and afford them prestige. Even in educational contexts, it is not uncommon to see entrepreneurial experiences explained in heroic terms. Contests, classes, and other entrepreneurship-learning exercises are promoted to students who see themselves (or want to be seen) as bold, passionate, and fast.

The presence of these external ideals can cause trouble for some entrepreneurial innovation teams. Gaining legitimacy and being perceived as competent are important tasks for teams in early phases of ascendancy. When teams, such as UhOhCo, attempt to act in ways that they imagine to be bold, passionate, and fast, they paradoxically can damage their chances for success. In other words, a team's efforts to act "entrepreneurially" can interfere with their abilities to respond authentically to their environment and make adaptations that would benefit their emerging product and strategy.

Let's look one more time at UhOhCo's exchange to find some examples of this phenomenon in action. Andy is absolute in his assessment of what is and is not important to the product and the venture. He is quick to defend the original vision when contrasting observations or ideas are presented. And he is oriented toward his personal stake – what he wants to create – rather than on a collaborative goal. Each of these details of his observable language suggests that he might be adhering to external ideals more than he is attending to the actual complexities of his team's current situation.

These external ideals about entrepreneurial traits can and do vex teams. Attempting to be bold, passionate, and fast can thwart a team's ability to recognize and grapple with the uncertainties of their actual experience.[4]

Because uncertainties are an integral part of the innovation process, all teams find ways of coping with them.[5] The full array of approaches can be located along two trajectories of mindfulness: the openness for new information and the ability to develop new evidence-based interpretations.[6] (See Figure 1.1.) One set of teams favors the reduction of uncertainty. They aim to gather abundant information and engage in lots of analysis to manage and control the uncertainties they perceive. Some other teams tend to deny uncertainty. They make a plan and execute it regardless of changing circumstances or new information. Still others acknowledge uncertainty and are open to change and feedback, but their inability to process that input limits the value they can glean from it. To compensate for that shortcoming, they try to predict changes and stay ahead of expected threats to their plan.

One last set of teams does not try to reduce, deny, or acknowledge uncertainty; they consciously enhance it. Through active tests of assumptions and through the language that they use in intra-team meetings they find ways to avoid premature cognitive commitments. These mindful actions allow them to productively adapt their products and strategies. These teams are the ones celebrated in the lean startup approach to entrepreneurship.

The lean startup approach advocates an iterative cycle with three main parts: building a prototype, measuring results of deliberate tests on the market's interest

FIGURE 1.1 Entrepreneurial stances toward uncertainties

in the latest version of the prototype, and adapting the prototype accordingly before testing assumptions about them again.[7] This learning cycle can enable a team to streamline the development of an initial product because it uses actual customer behaviors – not interviews, surveys, or wishful thinking – to guide the features that will be built.

Interpreting the feedback

It is tempting to think that feedback from customers is straightforward. If no one uses a certain feature of your product in a test perhaps that feature is not essential to the product's success. However, is that the only interpretation of the customer behavior? What if an interface design issue caused people to overlook that feature? Only by engaging in thoughtful discussions about the results of the test (followed sometimes by additional testing) can a team tease out the meaning(s) of feedback.

And this is where some teams, even those doing their best to follow the lean startup approach, can get stuck. If teams do not interpret the feedback well, they can make a long series of fruitless pivots. Similarly, if teams do not take the time to consider the various possible meanings of the feedback they have gotten they may not find the sweet spot between what the customer wants and what the team can deliver. In either case, such teams might feel frustrated and confused – they have followed the lean startup three-stage cycle, but they have not been able to get the traction that they seek in the market. They have spent time, money, social capital, and other resources going through the stages, but they are left with little to show for it.

Some have said that new venture failures tend to be caused by a team's premature commitment to the wrong course of action.[8,9] In fact, the lean startup movement is built on the idea that active testing of assumptions with prospective customers will prevent teams from overcommitting to unproductive paths. But it takes insight to determine which pivots will be the productive pivots, and insight does not always come as a eureka moment, as an effortless and fast cognitive snap. So despite the goal of increased speed that can come from the lean approach, the innovation teams that take time to collaboratively and deliberately interpret customer feedback tend to do better than the ones that rush forward.[10]

To be clear, successful teams are not leisurely; this is part of the reason why teams in accelerators do better than teams in incubators.[11] Successful teams are purposeful and deliberate in their quest to understand the possible meanings embedded in learning cycle feedback. However, they also take the time necessary to consider different ways of understanding the feedback, the time necessary to examine the biases they hold that might skew their ability to pivot productively. They recognize that the urge to be fast – to look confident and driven – can cheat teams out of the benefits that could emerge from interpretive conversations grounded in the data gathered from customers.[12]

Suffice it to say that the lean startup process is inherently social. It requires teams to engage in rich conversations in order to enact effective pivots even if that seems to temporarily slow the process of innovating. Boundaries between saying and doing get blurry in the innovation process because the conversations themselves are helping to make the innovations real. Moreover, the conversations are helping to make the markets for the innovation real as well. **Breakthrough products and new ventures are "talked into being" through layers of interactions between people.**[13]

Given that innovative products are brought to life, in part, through intrateam conversations, understanding how teams talk during the innovation process matters. It is important not because it would be nice to know. It is important because conversations can make the difference between success and failure. That means by thoughtfully attending to the structures of your team's innovation conversations you can increase your chances of success. Moreover, it is important because verbal skills can be learned. You cannot quickly change the technical skills or business acumen of your team (without adding new members), but you can increase your team's verbal abilities – and by extension your team's prospects for ascendancy – with relative ease.

A great example of the value that can come from developing your team's conversational competencies can be found in the aviation industry. Because the voice recorder – the so-called black box – aboard every airplane automatically captures all cockpit crew conversations, researchers have been able to identify verbal patterns that differentiate high- and low-performance crews. The research has shown that when facing the same human errors and technical malfunctions crews that talk in certain ways tend to land safely while crews that talk in other ways tend to crash. Consequently, training on the conversational moves that lead to greater flight safety has become required for most commercial airline crewmembers.[14,15] And airline safety has, in fact, improved.[16]

Of course, the conversational patterns that are associated with cockpit crew performance are not the same as those associated with innovative entrepreneurial team performance. But by using the same analytical techniques, recent research into the intra-team conversations of high-tech innovative entrepreneurial teams has yielded sets of specific conversational markers that tend to differentiate these teams based on performance (e.g., their ability to raise venture capital, release version 1.0 of their product, and function as a viable venture for at least 2 years).

One last thing . . .

Some entrepreneurs are motivated to start ventures because they believe that starting a venture means that they will have more control.[17] While some founders may get the independence they seek, many more come to find that leading a high-growth company means that they have to share control with teammates, investors, and other stakeholders.

The association of control with entrepreneurship can express itself in the contours of a team's interactions. For example, some founders who are motivated by control may dominate their team meetings. This can be true in terms of content; remember Andy from UhOhCo telling his teammates what *he* wants and expects the team to create. It also can be true in terms of conversational structure and turn taking. Sometimes lead entrepreneurs mistakenly think that they are entitled (or expected) to respond to every utterance in a team meeting. They mistakenly think that their team answers to them.

Teams that ascend typically have a more cooperative way of working. Rather than blindly doing the bidding of a lead entrepreneur, successful teams tend to develop a culture that encourages participation and interdependency. And while culture is more than language, the ways that teams talk shape circumstantial identities (e.g., provider of information, partner in celebration), social identities (e.g., lead entrepreneur, co-founder), and organizational identities (e.g., social venture, venture-backed team).[18,19] Moreover, the verbal skills of founders can help or hinder their ability to attract new teammates to an emerging venture.

When lead entrepreneurs persist in dominating conversations, they limit their team's ability to respond creatively. Without a conversational culture that allows people to think out loud about new information from customers, for example, a team will miss out on possible interpretations of that information. Consequently, the team might miss an important perspective that can lead to a productive pivot.

Getting to the good stuff

Fortunately, all the misperceptions that hamper innovative entrepreneurial teams can be identified and addressed in action. Teams can improve their chances of success by becoming aware of their habitual approaches and by developing new skills.

By raising your awareness about the role of conversation in the innovative entrepreneurial process this book aims to help your team understand how you might work more effectively together. Moreover, by articulating specific conversational moves that have been shown to enhance the interpretive process and improve innovative entrepreneurial team success, this book aims to help your team ascend.

The next chapter goes into greater detail about the language forms that have been associated with high- and low-performance innovative entrepreneurial teams. And future sections offer exercises and processes to help you build a successful venture by developing your conversational competencies.

Chapter takeaways

Traps that limit a team's performance	What it is	Tips on how to do better
Trying to act entrepreneurial	Trying to embody externally imposed ideals of boldness, passion, and speed may inhibit your team's success Trying to exert control over the team's processes may limit your team's agility and ability to attract additional teammates	Focus on the evidence that you are collecting from customers, advisors, and other relevant stakeholders. Focus on creating a collaborative culture.
Denying uncertainty	Trying to ignore uncertainty	Acknowledging ongoing uncertainty is better than denying it. Remind yourself that entrepreneurial work is inherently uncertain.
Reducing uncertainty	Imposing a false sense of certainty on a changing and complex situation	Acknowledging ongoing uncertainty is better than trying to contain or minimize it. Consciously expanding uncertainty – through words and experiments – is even better.

Questions for my team

Can we think of any instances in which we engaged in any of the three traps that can hamper innovative entrepreneurial performance?

Are there other myths about entrepreneurs and entrepreneurial work that have been influencing our approach?

How might we talk differently when we face similar circumstances in the future?

Notes

1 Bruner, J. (1996). Frames for thinking: Ways of meaning making. In D. Olson & N. Torrence (Eds.), *Modes of thought: Explorations in culture and cognition*. New York, NY: Cambridge University Press, 93–105.
2 Anderson, A. R., & Warren, L. (2011). The entrepreneur as hero and jester: Enacting the entrepreneurial discourse. *International Small Business Journal, 29*(6), 589–609.
3 Down, S., & Warren, L. (2008). Constructing narratives of enterprise: Cliche's and entrepreneurial self-identity. *International Journal of Entrepreneurial Behaviour and Research, 14*(1), 4–23.

4 Campbell, B. (2019). *Practice theory in action: Empirical studies of interaction in innovation and entrepreneurship*. New York, NY: Routledge.

5 Campbell, B. (2014). *Entrepreneurship as a conversational accomplishment: An inductive analysis of the verbal sensemaking behaviors of early-stage innovative entrepreneurial teams* (PhD). Exeter, England: University of Exeter.

6 Langer, E. J. (1989). *Mindfulness*. Reading, MA: Addison-Wesley Pub. Co.

7 Ries, E. (2011). *The lean startup*. New York, NY: Crown Business.

8 Ibid.

9 Furr, N., & Ahlstrom, P. (2011). *Nail it then scale it: The entrepreneur's guide to creating and managing breakthrough innovation*. UT: NISI Institute.

10 Lester, R. K., & Piore, M. J. (2004). *Innovation, the missing dimension*. Cambridge, MA: Harvard University Press.

11 Aulet, W. (2014). Avoid stagnation: Acceleration Trumps incubation. Paper presented at the SXSW, Austin, TX.

12 Campbell, B. (2019). *Practice theory in action: Empirical studies of interaction in innovation and entrepreneurship*. New York, NY: Routledge.

13 Heritage, J. (1984). *Garfinkel and ethnomethodology*. Cambridge: Polity Press.

14 Kanki, B. G., & Smith, G. M. (2001). Training aviation communication skills. In E. Salas, C. Bowers, & E. Edens (Eds.), *Improving teamwork in organizations*. Mahwah, NJ: Lawrence Erlbaum Associates, 95–127.

15 Nevile, M. (2004). *Beyond the black box: Talk-in-interaction in the airline cockpit*. Ashgate.

16 Tuccio, W., & Nevile, M. (2017). Using conversation analysis in data-driven aviation training with large-scale qualitative datasets. *Journal of Aviation/Aerospace Education & Research*, *26*(1), 1.

17 Kelley, D., Ali, A., Brush, C., Corbett, A., Daniels, C., Kim, P., Rogoff, E. (2016). Global entrepreneurship monitor: 2015. United States Report: Babson College and Baruch College.

18 Schegloff, E. A. (1992). Repair after next turn: The last structurally provided defense of intersubjectivity in conversation. *American Journal of Sociology*, *97*(5), 1295–1345.

19 Schegloff, E. A. (2007). *Sequence organization in interaction: A primer in conversation analysis* (Vol. 1). Cambridge: Cambridge University Press.

2

WHY POPULAR APPROACHES TO INNOVATION AREN'T ENOUGH

Knowing what to do is different from knowing how to do it

Some of the best-selling business books in recent years have been written to improve the performance of high-tech innovation teams, especially high-tech, high-growth entrepreneurial innovation teams. Perhaps you have read some of them. Perhaps you have changed your team's routines to incorporate some of their recommended processes. And perhaps your team is still not performing at the level you would like.

There are many different ways to approach the innovation process. Lean startup methodology, human-centered design, design thinking, and agile development are a few approaches that you might recognize. Although they each have their own terminology and nuanced descriptions of the innovation process, they all share the idea that better innovation occurs through grounded observation and prototype iteration. Consequently, I could draw from any of these observational approaches to anchor several key points. However, for the sake of simplicity, I will focus on the lean startup approach for explanations and examples in this book. It seems to be the most widely adopted of the observational approaches to innovation; it is taught at more than 25 universities and is the cornerstone of many accelerators and business model contests around the world.[1]

A summary of the lean startup approach would have to start with a description of *The Lean Startup* book. Based on the professional experience of Eric Ries and his interviews with other innovative entrepreneurs, *The Lean Startup* posits a theory of entrepreneurial success based on iterative experiments and team learning.[2] It acknowledges that entrepreneurs are surrounded by uncertainty and suggests that the optimal means for functioning within such circumstances is to deliberately test assumptions about a team's vision for a new product. The author advocates a three-phase cycle for testing assumptions: build a minimal prototype, offer it to prospective customers, and adapt the prototype based on customer reaction to it. This process is iterative, and it may cause teams to pivot before they can succeed, to make a significant change to the product, customer base, or strategy in order to ascend. In the end, successful teams will engage in the iterative learning cycle, emerge with a minimum viable product, and eventually achieve market success.

This approach to innovative entrepreneurial work offers many advantages to people intent on building a venture. However, it – like every approach to innovation – has some limitations or unintended consequences. One potential snag is the emphasis on speed. For example, a primary reason for a team choosing to adopt a lean startup approach is to get better results faster: to iteratively go through the build–measure–learn loop in a quest to create a minimum viable product as quickly as possible. The pressure for entrepreneurial innovation teams to be fast is one of the triggers outlined in the previous chapter. As tempting as it is to assume that faster is better, the truth is that the perceived need to act fast can lead teams down some unproductive paths that unintentionally consume time, money, and all other resources.

Another shortcoming shared by the observational methods for entrepreneurial innovation is that they only describe the workflow, the phases that teams go through while crafting a product and starting a venture. For example, the lean startup approach explains that successful teams experiment, evaluate the results of those experiments, and alter their prototypes before repeating the process. While these descriptions of workflow are insightful and helpful, they fail to tell you one critical thing. **As clearly as they might be able to tell you *what* to do these descriptions of workflow do not tell you *how* to do it.**

This gap between understanding what and knowing how is important.

The interpretive aspects of entrepreneurial work

There is tremendous variety in how entrepreneurial teams enact a lean startup approach to innovation. It is not that they fail to understand the principles of the lean startup approach; the members of both high- and low-performance teams can explain the build–measure–learn cycle, for example. And it is not that they are careless in their application of the principles; the teams at both ends of the performance spectrum are genuinely attempting to incorporate the recommended lean startup steps into their practice. Nevertheless, there is a noticeable difference in the ways that teams perform the steps, differences that seem to align with their levels of eventual success.

Innovation is a highly social act. The lean startup approach emphasizes the dynamic human element by stressing the importance of a team's ability to process sought-after and unbidden data on customer behavior. But the lean startup approach does not deeply explore or explain the ways that teams grapple with the information and insights that they gather, how they transform data and surprises into progress. Advocates for the lean startup approach recognize that all teams accomplish some of their work in meetings – which teams surely do. But they also tend to assume that all teams interact in the same ways in those meetings – which teams do not. Many of the observational approaches to innovation wrongly imagine that all teams know how to optimally exchange information, interpret observations, and plan courses of action in meetings.

Because a large part of innovation is social in nature it is important to understand how the interpersonal and interpretative parts of the process work. The trouble is: discovering how teams enact a lean startup practice is not easy. You cannot uncover the *how* of a team's work by interviewing them or asking them to participate in a survey. You also cannot uncover the how of a successful innovation process by simply watching teams work in real time. Instead, it takes a micro-analytical and comparative approach to reveal the underlying interactional mechanisms that enable some lean startup teams to succeed while others fail.

In my research with teams around the world, I have attempted to uncover the *how* of innovation. I have taken a very close look at the social practices and verbal mechanisms that teams use to enact the lean startup method. A later section of this book explains the details of the research traditions that inform my research, but for now the main thing you need to know is that I have studied the language forms that teams use in their intra-team conversations when they are building minimum viable products and launching innovative new ventures. I have studied how teams at both ends of the performance spectrum talk (or try to talk) their innovations into being.

The primary discovery from that research: high- and low-performance teams interact differently with each other while engaged in the lean startup process. Both high- and low-performance teams attend to the recommended steps and procedures such as developing minimally and testing hypothesis frequently. However, while all teams go through the phases of the lean startup learning cycle, they do so very differently. In particular, the interpretive aspects – the interactions that give rise to new ideas and insights based on the results of the lean startup experiments – vary significantly between the teams that perform well and the teams that do not. The conversational differences between the teams turn out to be tightly aligned with early-stage performance metrics such as raising money, building a capable team, and releasing a successful product.

When the naturally-occurring conversations of lean startup teams are analyzed, the results show that teams devote a lot of their meetings to interpreting their observations of customer behavior. Some portion of meetings is focused on exchanging information and articulating plans for action. However, when a team is engaged in the process of creating a minimum viable product, they devote most of their conversations to making sense of the results of their experiments with customers. Specifically, according to one study, teams talking about crafting a minimum viable product devote 42% of their utterances to ascribing meaning, 36% to exchanging information, and 22% to expressing possible courses of action.[3]

In other words, crafting a minimum viable product is not only a technical feat or even a social act; it is also an interpretive act. Lean startup teams spend a significant amount of time and energy making sense of their innovation: trying to understand what they're doing, how they're doing it, and why.[4] Whether they are comparing two conflicting pieces of data from the experiments or comparing data from customer experiments with their preexisting vision for the innovation, lean startup teams must grapple with the meanings to assign to their observations when they are developing minimum viable products.

Not surprisingly, there are distinct conversational differences that separate the successful teams from the rest. High-performance lean startup teams tend to use language that expands their opportunities to explore an array of interpretations about their situation more than low-performance teams do. In particular, their conversations tend to be marked with language that is collaborative, provisional, and reflective. One of the primary benefits of these flexible language forms – of framing situations with "could be" rather than "is", for example, or using levity to play with absurd possibilities – is that they can protect a team from making premature commitments to faulty interpretations and suboptimal courses of action.

Interpretive language forms express plausibility rather than precision. Using them enables lean startup teams to maintain an inquisitive stance toward their work and to function productively in the near term while retaining open options for the longer term. Given that the ability to make progress amid uncertainties is essential to an entrepreneurial team's success, anything that can help a team accomplish that is worth cultivating. And the frequent use of these interpretive language forms seems to give teams an edge.

Low-performance teams tend to communicate differently in their meetings.[5] They are prone to having conversations that lack coherence. Rather than building on each other's ideas, teammates redirect the conversation onto new trajectories. Or rather than building on the data that have emerged from the lean startup experiments, teammates introduce new ideas (i.e., brainstorms) that are disconnected from the customer feedback. The result of these random interruptions is an unsatisfying and unproductive meeting in which lots of ideas and opinions have been offered but no actionable, shared insights have emerged.

Unproductive meetings lacking in actionable, shared insights can be the outcome of another conversational trait of low-performance teams: polarized positions. Rather than really considering what another person is saying, members of low-performance teams tend to act as if they already know what a teammate is going to say. Compounding this listening failure is the possibility that some teammates may have brittle ideas about a product feature, for example, that the frequently evangelize. This dynamic leads to a paralyzed exchange and no progress on the key issues facing the team.

Low-performance teams also are likely to fall into other kinds of conversational ruts. Their team meetings are susceptible to become mired in groupthink – a social phenomenon driven primarily by a team's desire to minimize conflict. In their attempts to keep the peace, team members restrict the exploration and thoughtful evaluation of alternative interpretations of their shared situation. They do so by actively suppressing dissenting viewpoints and hedging their own ideas.

Despite their struggles and lack of success, low-performance teams are still well-intended teams. They can sense the presence of teamwork challenges, and they take efforts to improve their meetings. Many import techniques from management consulting in an attempt to improve their productivity. Outcomes-based agendas, for example, may be tried to enable a team to define the content and end point of its meetings in advance. Tools of this kind deliver efficiency, and a streamlined meeting might feel better to the participants. However, tools that restrict unwanted exchanges and predetermine end points often diminish constructive exploration and expansion too.

Language as a tool

Management tools and techniques that limit uncertainties can give teams a false sense of progress. Distracted by the illusion of momentum, teams will continue to execute a flawed plan long after the evidence in their environment would have indicated a need to change course. In other words, while teams might enjoy more efficient meetings, efficiency is rarely the main cause of disappointing performance for innovative entrepreneurial teams. Instead, teams need to grapple with the dynamic circumstances and ambiguous information that define the entrepreneurial experience; they need to find ways to productively interpret the uncertainties that surround them.

Language is a different kind of tool, one that all teams use for better or worse. Language can help teams interpret uncertainties if they use it in advantageous ways. For example, as later chapters will explain, framing situations in conditional ways – using might be in instead of must be or is – is a linguistic mechanism that seems to protect teams from premature cognitive commitments to product features or courses of action. Low-performance teams, however, tend to rely on language that does them more harm than good. In their product validation meetings, for example, they often rely on language that expresses a definitive, unyielding, and absolute point of view.

Teams that make frequent use of inflexible language might have a very difficult time ascending. Minimizing uncertainties in order to make what feels like progress is a poor strategy for success. Like outcomes-based agendas, inflexible language can move a team to premature closure on topics that require protracted considerations. When a team's language reduces or denies the complexities of their actual situation the team cannot make good choices about the next steps to take. The better linguistic option is to acknowledge (and even expand through hypothetical conversation) the uncertainty, to verbally accept the disruptions that emerge when undertaking the challenge of innovative entrepreneurship.

Although most aspiring entrepreneurs are encouraged to be disruptive – to ask disruptive questions, to build products that disrupt a market, and so on – few teams are coached on how to handle the disruptions that will happen inevitably to them. Formal course work in entrepreneurship has tended to focus on the development of skills related analysis and planning, for example, how to do sensitivity analyses, predictive financials, and business-plan writing. More practice-based learning experiences expose aspiring entrepreneurs to customer interactions and encourage them to build a team with expert teammates and capable advisors. Course work and connections with key people can help teams prepare for (and ideally avoid) predictable surprises.[6] However, they do little to help teams consciously develop interpretive skills; the skills that will enable them to deal in real-time with unexpected, unwanted, and unsettling information or events.

Analytical skills are, of course, extremely valuable for innovative entrepreneurial teams to master. They provide the foundation for organizational stability and defensible decision making. However, these skills need to be in balance with interpretive skills in order for a team to reach its full potential. When working from an analytical stance a team is likely to think in problem-solving mode. They are likely to strive to develop a logical solution as quickly as possible and move on. A team working from an interpretive stance is likely to have a different approach. They are likely to look for different ways to understand the challenge facing them before engaging in an iterative process of design. The interpretive process strives not to reach quick closure but to articulate a range of alternative possibilities for consideration based on the evidence available.

Eventually the analytical skills prevail; a team must choose a specific course of action that can be executed (and explained to the board of directors eventually) in cost-effective and time-effective ways. However, the richer the array of alternative options available for consideration the more likely the team will select a promising direction.

There are some key differences between an analytical and an interpretive approach to innovative entrepreneurial work.[7] Analytical approaches work best when applied to a project with a clear beginning and end point. In other words, they are best suited for discrete problem-solving. Analytically oriented meetings aim to resolve differences in perspective and to eliminate ambiguities. They are goal-driven and use conversation to exchange specific pieces of information. In contrast, interpretive approaches are a process rather than a project. They are emergent and iterative in nature, and they help teams uncover new meanings and options. Meetings with an interpretive orientation encourage different viewpoints and explore ambiguities. They are focused on meaning-making and use conversation to expand a team's awareness of assumptions and possible next steps.

Because interpretative conversations are important to the work of entrepreneurial innovation teams, it makes sense to examine the contours of teams' conversations. The next section of this book explains the conversational competencies of entrepreneurial innovation teams in detail. It clarifies what interpretive language forms are, and how successful teams employ collaborative, provisional, and reflective conversational moves to enact their work. It goes beyond the descriptions of *what* lean startup teams do; it shows you in detail *how* lean startup teams verbally accomplish their goals.

VERBAL MOVES AND TEAM OUTCOMES

The verbal profiles of high- and low-performance teams enacting lean startup approaches to innovative entrepreneurship do differ. But what constitutes performance?

In one of my studies, the naturally occurring language used by teams in their intra-team meetings was recorded over an 8- to 12-week period. These were early-stage founding teams that had recently begun an accelerator program. None of them had incorporated or created a functioning prototype yet. All of them had access to an advisory network, office space, and a small cushion of cash ($1,000). None of the teams had worked together before. All the teams had functional diversity (e.g., a person with technical expertise, a person with business expertise, etc.). In other words, at the time of the data collection, all the participating teams seemed as equal as they could be in their chances for success.

The analysis of the data found that a subset of the teams (two out of six) had language profiles that looked similar to the profiles of high-performance teams; they frequently used collaborative, provisional, and reflective language. The analysis also showed that most of the teams did not have verbal profiles that looked like those of high-performance teams. One of those two teams won an award at the end of the accelerator, and the other was a finalist for an award.

Two years later, both of the teams whose verbal profiles suggested that they might become high-performance teams had incorporated and were building their ventures. They collectively had raised more than $5 million. They had hired employees, won recognition, and built customer bases for real product offerings. They were, by the standards of most early-stage entrepreneurs and entrepreneurship educators, successful. Of course, each of them had a long way to go before their exit strategies could be realized. But as evaluations of innovative entrepreneurial ventures go, these teams were successful in accomplishing the critical first milestones of ascendancy.

The teams whose verbal profiles did not include frequent use of collaborative, provisional, and reflective language did not fare as well. Two years after the data was collected none of those teams existed. They had all disbanded even though some were still hopeful about a possible future for their envisioned yet dormant product concept. They were not successful by the traditional measures of entrepreneurial performance.

Closing comments

This chapter and the one before it have articulated some of the limitations of conventional approaches to innovative entrepreneurship. When teams believe that they can achieve success just by embodying external ideals about entrepreneurship and surrounding themselves with experts then the sources of mainstream guidance have let teams down.

Your stance toward uncertainty does matter. If your team is oriented toward reducing, denying, or just passively accepting uncertainty, then you might be in for a difficult experience as an innovative entrepreneurial team. If, on the other hand, your team is comfortable expanding uncertainty in thoughtful ways – through conversational moves that enable you to protract interpretive opportunities – then you might be poised for greater success.

Conversation is the main way that teams grapple productively with uncertainty, how they exchange information, ascribe meaning, and define next steps. While you cannot perfectly control or predict the uncertain dynamics of an entrepreneurial endeavor you can develop the conversational abilities to productively deal with whatever challenges emerge. Several key conversational moves have been associated with high-performance innovative entrepreneurial teams. Collaborative, provisional, and reflective language helps teams to recognize alternative possibilities, to make progress while avoiding premature cognitive commitments. The next set of chapters introduce the fundamentals of each of these language forms to you.

Chapter takeaways

Dynamics that can hinder performance	What it is	Tips on how to do better
Incoherence, groupthink, and polarized positions	Meeting dynamics that are marked by disjointed conversations, a desire to avoid discord, or an inability to listen appreciatively	Set norms and model behaviors for meetings that encourage teammates to grapple with the specifics of their shared challenges.
Fixed, inflexible language	Imposing too much certainty on a situation; absolute verb forms such as *must be* tend to play a role.	Remember that there could be other explanations that the first one that seems to fit. Flexible words such as *possibly* or *might* tend to help achieve this.
Overreliance on analytical skills and underdeveloped interpretative skills	Approaching every issue as a problem to be solved as quickly possible	Search for good ways to find good solutions rather than honing in on the single best way forward.

Questions for my team

How often are our team meetings oriented toward finding *the* answer (rather than finding a good way to find a reasonably good solution)?

How much time do we devote to considering various perspectives and options before selecting a course of action? Is it enough? Is it too much?

Do we sometimes impose a false certainty on our situation? Are we disciplined about saying *might* or *could* to indicate healthy levels of doubt?

Notes

1 Blank, S. (2013). Why the lean startup changes everything. *Harvard Business Review*, *91*(5), 63–72.
2 Ries, E. (2011). *The lean startup.* New York, NY: Crown Business.
3 Campbell, B. (2014). *Entrepreneurship as a conversational accomplishment: An inductive analysis of the verbal sensemaking behaviors of early-stage innovative entrepreneurial teams* (PhD). Exeter, England: University of Exeter.
4 Mezirow, J. (1991). *Transformative dimensions of adult learning.* San Francisco, CA: Jossey-Bass.
5 Perkins, D. N. (2003). *King Arthur's round table: How collaborative conversations create smart organizations.* Wiley.
6 Bazerman, M., & Watkins, M. (2004). *Predictable surprises: The disasters you should have seen coming, and how to prevent them.* Boston, MA: Harvard Business Press.
7 Lester, R. K., & Piore, M. J. (2004). *Innovation, the missing dimension.* Cambridge, MA: Harvard University Press.

PART 2
Explaining interpretive language

High- and low-performance innovative entrepreneurial teams tend to use different language forms when engaged in conversations at work. In general, high-performance teams tend to use language that is more flexible than low-performance teams do. In particular, they tend to use language that is collaborative, provisional, and reflective. These conversational moves allow teams to dwell in an interpretive stance, a behavior that seems to lead to more productive pivots and better long-term success. And as you might expect, the conversational practices that low-performance teams use tend to be quite different. This section explains the key conversational practices of teams at both ends of the performance spectrum.

3

COLLABORATIVE LANGUAGE

It's all about the quality of conversation

Everyone, it seems, is in favor of collaboration. For decades, the merits of teamwork have been touted by scholars, management consultants, and business leaders. However, all too often, teams only "co-blabberate".[1] Instead of engaging in real collaboration, many teams simply talk about the value of teamwork and fail to build practices that harness the contributions of the team members and advance their shared goals. However, those teams that can cultivate a truly collaborative way of working together position themselves to ascend.

Organizing work to maximize the interdependencies between team members is one way that teams create a culture of collaboration.[2,3] Unlike the old assembly-line approach to work, a model for interdependent work does not restrict workers to focusing on discrete tasks. Instead, the structure of interdependent work requires all team members to understand and influence the big picture. Everyone needs to be able to recognize how their daily efforts add up to the end result. Moreover, everyone needs to be able to talk about self-concordant goals, to express how their individual responsibilities align with the team's shared objective.

Collaboration also is supported by the turn-taking structure of team conversations. For example, teams that discuss the insights or information offered by teammates outperform teams that ignore or quickly reject each other's contributions. Similarly, teams that take time to ask clarifying questions and explore the points that have been raised by teammates do better than those whose conversations skip abruptly from topic to topic. Moreover, team performance is associated with these interactional profiles regardless of the prior achievements of the individual team members.[4]

The quantity of conversation also has been linked with better collaboration and better outcomes. Higher-performing teams simply talk more with each other – in terms of words spoken in a given conversation and frequency of conversations – than lower-performing teams. This could be because the more collaborative and successful teams are made up of friends. Or it could be that the act of communicating with each other builds familiarity and trust which facilitate better integration of tasks and more successful outcomes.[5]

Simply put, collaboration is based in and can be enhanced by verbal interaction. A deeper look into the conversational moves of innovative entrepreneurial teams, in particular, suggests that collaboration – and eventually performance – is associated with frequent use of the first-person plural, heedful ways of interacting with team members, and equal participation between team members in meetings.

The power of pronouns

To understand the value of the first-person plural to the success of an innovation team, it might be useful to begin by reviewing some fundamentals of grammar. The English language has many types of personal pronouns. (See Table 3.1.) Some are singular, some are plural, and they all express a relational point of view. For example, first-person pronouns indicate a connection with the speaker (i.e., the one who is speaking for him- or herself or for his or her group). Second-person pronouns indicate a separation from the speaker (i.e., the person or group who is being spoken to). Third-person pronouns indicate a distance from the speaker and the listener (i.e., the person or group who is being spoken about). There are other aspects of personal pronouns, of course. However, the first-person plural (e.g., we, us, our) is what warrants attention for our purposes.

In his book, *The Secret Life of Pronouns: What Our Words Say about Us*, linguist James Pennebaker[6] reveals how high-functioning teams use pronouns. In general, the use of the first-person plural is associated with teams that get along well. Pennebaker posits that teams that use more we-language tend to have thicker bonds with each other and a stronger identity with the work that brings them together. The culture of connectedness that results from a team's inclusive language (and other gestures that are addressed in later sections of this book) contributes to a positive cycle of productivity and achievement. On the other hand, higher usage of the second person – *you*, either singular or plural – might be an indicator of relational distance or discord among team members.

TABLE 3.1 Personal pronouns

	SINGULAR			PLURAL		
	Subjective	*Objective*	*Possessive*	*Subjective*	*Objective*	*Possessive*
1st person	I	me	my, mine	*we*	*us*	*our, ours*
2nd person	you	you	your, yours	you	you	your, yours
3rd person	he, she, it	him, her, it	his, hers, its	they	them	their, theirs

To do this work, Pennebaker along with his co-workers developed text analysis software program called Linguistic Inquiry and Word Count (LIWC).[7,8] The software analyzes transcriptions of verbal communication on a word-by-word basis and calculates the percentage of words in the file that match particular dimensions of language. Linguistic dimensions that can be measured include many categories such as word count, verb tense, and pronouns.

Following in Pennebaker's footsteps, other researchers have used the LIWC to investigate the language used by cockpit crews in action. This stream of research supports the idea that better performing teams tend to use the first-person plural more frequently than poorly performing teams.[9] In one key study, cockpit crews that had the safest outcomes and fewest errors in the flight simulator were those that used first-person plural pronouns the most often.

While lean startup teams don't have the same kinds of safety concerns as cockpit crews, all too many of them do crash and burn, to use a common turn of phrase. Inspired by Pennebaker's work and the research into cockpit crews, in particular, I began to wonder if successful high-tech innovative entrepreneurial teams would also use *we*, *us*, and *our* more often than their less successful peers.

Curious, I decided to experiment with LIWC. My cursory investigation began with recordings from a set of early-stage innovative entrepreneurial teams. After gathering more than thirty hours of naturally occurring conversations from these teams at work, I transcribed their conversations and analyzed them with the LIWC. Two years later, I followed up with those teams. The teams that used the most first-person plural in their early-stage team meetings had become real companies that had raised money, built product, and had revenue from real customers. The teams that used the first-person plural the least had abandoned their ventures.

Heedfulness

In addition to telling us about team identity, the use of the first-person plural signals the possible presence of heedful interactions – another important marker associated with high-performance teams. Just as the use of *we*-words can improve a team's sense of shared identity, engaging in heedful interactions can improve a team's sense of collective efficacy.[10,11]

Heedful interactions are respectful and mutually supportive exchanges. Team members responding heedfully attend to the conversation as it is happening in thoughtful and purposeful ways. In other words, when interacting heedfully, you resist the temptation to assume you know what someone else is going to say. You empathize with the positions and contributions of teammates and shape your own actions to complement the efforts of the team.[12] Some even go so far as to say that the subordination of individual aspirations in favor of shared success is the hallmark of heedful relating – and that the ability to defer to the good of the team is a primary driver of successful team-based innovation.[13]

To illustrate how a successful innovative entrepreneurial team chooses shared goals over individual visions, let's take a look at an exchange between the members of a venture named TopCo. Sherri and Jack are co-founders of an early-stage high-tech company. They have been adhering to a lean startup approach during the few months that they have worked together. Here is an excerpt from a conversation about an upcoming demo for their product.

Excerpt 3.1

Sherri	I think it would be really fun if we had a picnic style tablecloth covering the table at the booth. Do you think that that's good, or is it just taking it just a bit too far? A little kitschy?
Jack	Maybe (tilting his head from side to side)
Sherri	Okay, we don't need the tablecloth. I can let that dream die.
Jack	If we had more food and maybe some ducks, you know!
Both	(laughter)
Sherri	Yeah, it is fun, but it might be a distraction. Should we have a signup sheet? A piece of paper for people to put their contact information if they're interested?
Jack	Get their names and all? And like directing them to our website for more info?
Sherri	Yeah.
Jack	Yeah, yeah, let's. Good idea.

While this might be an easy negotiation – neither person is terribly invested in the tablecloth and the decision about it is unlikely to impact the venture in any significant way – it does reveal how teammates heedfully manage individual and shared goals. Sherri has a vision that includes a playful tablecloth at an industry event. She also has an awareness that her partner's perspective matters, and she initiates a request for his feedback on something she would like to do. He offers an honest answer that includes some appreciation for her idea in the form of a playful quip. And Sherri is able to yield to his perspective; she decides that they don't really need the tablecloth even though she would have liked it.

These two teammates anticipate each other's needs by volunteering explanations before miscommunications can occur. When Sherri clarifies that by "signup sheet", she means "a piece of paper for people to put their contact information"; she is ensuring clear communication and is expressing respect for the relationship and its shared goals.

Another heedful thing to notice is that Sherri and Jack are polite but not excessively so. Jack's indirect answer ("maybe") is a form of politeness. Indirect speech, such as his in this instance, indicates mutual respect; it helps a partner save face. High-performance teams tend to use indirect speech in this way more often than low-performance teams. However, indirect speech also can be used as a hedge that weakens a statement's strength. When used in this manner, indirect speech protects the *speaker* and suggests unequal status among teammates. Hedges are used more often by low-performance teams.[14,15,16]

For teammates to be able to speak up – to feel no need to hedge and protect the self – they must feel psychologically safe within the context of their team.[17] Psychological safety includes beliefs about the ways that teammates will respond when one asks questions, seeks feedback, reports errors, or proposes new ideas. If team members believe that they can speak freely without a fear of humiliation or other negative consequences, then a workplace is considered to be psychologically safe.

Equal participation

Team members who work in a psychologically safe environment tend to seek feedback, seek help, and share concerns with each other more freely than team members in less-secure circumstances.[18] Moreover, they tend to engage in these exchanges in equal measure; that is, their conversations include nearly equal participation among team members.

For a quick example of a high-performance team seeking feedback take another look at the conversation between TopCo's Sherri and Jack from a few pages ago. Sherri is asking Jack directly for Jack's opinion about the tablecloth. She doesn't hide from sharing a creative idea, nor does she assume he'll like it. In the collaborative context of their shared work, Sherri can request honest feedback from Jack without hesitation.

High-performance teams also seek help from each other (and from relevant people across the ecosystem). Asking for help means that a speaker must reveal a lack of knowledge, something that might be difficult to do in a psychologically unsafe context. Again, the high-performance TopCo team can provide an example of this kind of exchange.

Excerpt 3.2

Jack　What's the term again? End use . . .
Sherri　End user profile; build an end user profile.
Jack　Got it.

In this instance Jack discloses his unfamiliarity with a standard business concept – an end-user profile. He unselfconsciously asks Sherri to remind him of the term so that they can make progress on their go-to-market plan. If he were concerned about hiding his ignorance it is easy to imagine that the team's productivity would temporarily fall while he tried to act as if he understood their shared task.

A psychologically safe environment also makes it easier for teammates to share concerns. Whether questioning their own abilities or other people's guidance, teams that have the benefit of psychological safety can explore the edges of ideas as TopCo's Sherri and Jack are able to do.

Excerpt 3.3

Sherri   One thing that our advisory board said was that they don't think that we're going to sell that many.

Jack   Yeah There's always that risk.

Sherri   Of course, but I just have a hard time with their assessment given all the interview data we have from people in our target market.

Jack   Yeah I agree . . .

Sherri   We have real people telling us that they want this. That they would buy and use this.

Jack   And we know there are more like them . . . Like 1 in 100, right?

Sherri   Yeah, somewhere between 1 in 100 and 1 in 170 people.

Each of these types of discourse – help seeking, help giving, and concern sharing – invite participation. In the case of Sherri and Jack, a two-person team, you would expect them to have an equal number of turns in the conversation. However, would you also expect them to contribute an equal number of words to the entire conversation? What about an equal number of direct questions? It turns out that high-performance teams have very balanced profiles of participation even at these very granular levels.

The balanced word counts evidenced by high-performance teams suggest the presence of a virtual role system. That is a fancy term that means the team members have a shared mental model about the organization, its internal roles, and its place in the wider world. Teams with a virtual role system are able to step in for each other if someone is absent, either temporarily or permanently. For example, if the teammate who usually provides some financial updates is going to have to miss a meeting, a different team member will recognize the importance of that contribution and will gather and report the information. This role redundancy is considered to be a hallmark of a virtual role system in action.[19,20] Teams that have such a common understanding of who and how they work as a unit tend to be more resilient in the face of uncertainty. Consequently, they tend to be more successful.

Creating a psychologically safe workplace

Simply put, the freedom and ease that come with psychologically safe workplaces have been associated with more and better innovation.[21] When teammates sense that their physical and emotional well-being is important at work, it enables them to express talents and ideas without the fear of any negative consequences.[22] Yet a challenge exists for teams: How can you create this kind of positive workplace with your teammates? Fortunately several simple behaviors can contribute to the cultivation of a psychologically safe workplace.[23,24]

First, openly acknowledge that the work of an innovative entrepreneurial team is full of uncertainty. Given that no one can know with certainty what is going to happen and what is going to work, every team member's assessments and input matters. Moreover, because of the high levels of uncertainty in innovative entrepreneurial work, everyone on the team needs to be ready to adapt. As circumstances change and new insights come into focus, the team must be ready to exchange an old, outdated vision for a new updated one. Establishing the team's shared goals as a matter of learning and discovery rather than of execution and performance invites engagement and involvement.

Second, as a leader, candidly reveal your own limitations and blunders (and encourage others to do the same). By communicating that you don't have perfect information or insight you enable other people to be honest about their shortcomings and to openly discuss errors that might happen along the way. When others reveal their limitations or mistakes, you can support them by demonstrating that you appreciate their honesty and understand how they feel. By creating these authentic channels of respectful interaction, you enable your team to act and even make mistakes without fear.

And third, demonstrate curiosity. By modeling a sincere interest in the information and interpretations that other team members hold, you welcome everyone into the discussion. Curiosity comes across when you ask open-ended questions that enable the other person to answer as authentically and richly as possible. It also is supported by clarifying questions that help you make sure you've understood what the other person was communicating. Demonstrating and supporting curiosity fosters the development of positive relationships and productive interdependencies between teammates.

When teams lack collaborative language

Because collaborative language is not difficult – it is a perfectly ordinary means of conducting conversations – many of us might assume that all teams communicate with each other in this manner. Unfortunately, most teams are not high-performance teams, and they communicate using less-collaborative language forms. In fact, the language used by low-performance teams in their meetings tends to be marked by several features:

- Reliance on first-person singular pronouns
- Expressions of disregard
- Patterns of uneven participation

When team members frequently use *I*, *me*, and *mine* instead of the first-person plural forms of pronouns they can limit themselves to a practice of parallel play and miss the benefits of real teamwork. Take this excerpt from a conversation by the low-performing UhOhCo as an example.

Excerpt 3.4

Andy   I don't know I'm just like – do I want to stay focused on the initial market segment or is there a bigger, better opportunity to go after like in the general medical record space?

Carol   I've been thinking that if the focus stays on the dental record segment we'll be more efficient.

Bridgette So I want to make sure I share this before I forget. Remember I was telling you about that shopping site that I used to love? So I found that site on the way back machine as it used to be when I liked it, and you have to see the interface . . .

Even though Andy, Carol, and Bridgette are on the same team they each are focused on their individual interests only. While they are speaking to each other, they are not building on each other's perspectives. Their language suggests that they lack a sense of interdependence and the ability to listen to and incorporate each other's efforts.

Their pronoun use amplifies their disregard for each other's contributions. By disregard I mean prideful statements that convey a speaker's belief that he or she knows best. By asserting that he or she knows better than a teammate or better than prospective customers, a team member effectively shuts down the conversation. Another form of disregard is expressed by claims that a speaker has accomplished more than other teammates (or competitors) and therefore knows best. Instead of inspiring the evolution of the team's minimum viable product, expressions of disregard inhibit the process of evidence-based innovation by shutting out team member contributions.

Quite literally, low-performance teams shut out some voices by maintaining unbalanced patterns of participation in team meetings. Sometimes a lead entrepreneur has a reply for every comment made by a team member as if everyone were speaking only to him or her. In other cases, one part of the team engages in conversation while another part of the team passively observes the meeting without verbally participating in it. And then there are teams that have meetings that regularly dissolve into several disconnected conversations at once.

When team members interact in these non-collaborative ways their actions erode a team's sense of shared efficacy. Using first-person singular pronouns, expressions of disregard, and uneven levels of participation can undermine the potential power of an innovative entrepreneurial team.

Part of a collection

Collaboration emerges through team interaction – especially conversation. The conversational moves highlighted in this chapter can help teams work together more effectively. Interactional markers that facilitate collaboration – such as the use of the first-person plural, heedfulness, and equal participation between team members in meetings – can support a team's ability to productively interpret the uncertainties of entrepreneurial work.

However, collaborative language is only one of the conversational competencies that innovative entrepreneurial teams need to master. The other two – provisional and reflective language – are the focus of the next chapters in this section of the book.

Chapter takeaways

Collaborative Conversational Competencies	What it is	Tips on how to cultivate
First-person plural	Pronouns including *we*, *us*, and *our*	Focus on the shared nature of the work.
Heedfulness	Respecting each other, incorporating the ideas of others	Seek feedback, seek help, and share concerns.
Equal participation	Balanced turn taking between teammates; also balanced word count and functioning virtual role systems	Cultivate psychological safety by framing the team's work as a learning task, recognizing limitations, and modeling curiosity. Expressly invite teammates to share their views with open-ended and clarifying questions.

Questions for my team

How often do we use the first-person plural? Does one of us use it more than the other(s)?

What about seeking opinions or help? How often do we each engage in those conversational gestures?

How are we with turn taking? How often do we ask open-ended and clarifying questions of each other?

How comfortable are we with acknowledging our individual and collective limitations?

Notes

1 Perkins, D. (2003). *King Arthur's round table: How collaborative conversations create smart organizations.* Wiley.
2 Hackman, J. (2002). *Leading teams: Setting the stage for great performances.* Boston, MA: Harvard Business School Press.

3 Wageman, R., & Gordon, F. (2005). As the twig is bent: How group values shape emergent task interdependence in groups. *Organizational Science, 16*(6), 687–700.

4 Barron, B. (2003). When smart groups fail. *The Journal of the Learning Sciences, 12*(3), 307–359.

5 Ibid.

6 Pennebaker, J. (2011). *The secret life of pronouns: What our words say about us.* New York, NY: Bloomsbury Press.

7 Pennebaker, J., Booth, R., & Francis, M. (2007). *Linguistic inquiry and word count: LIWC.* Austin, TX: LIWC.

8 Tausczik, Y., & Pennebaker, J. (2010). The psychological meaning of words: LIWC and computerized text analysis methods. *Journal of Language and Social Psychology, 29*(1), 24–54.

9 Sexton, J., & Helmreich, R. (2003). Using language in the cockpit: Relationships with workload and performance. In R. Dietrich (Ed.), *Communication in high risk environments* (Vol. Special issue 12). Hamburg: Buske, 57–74.

10 Bandura, A., & Locke, E. (2003). Negative self-efficacy and goal effects revisited. *Journal of Applied Psychology, 88*(1), 87.

11 Sutcliffe, K., & Vogus, T. (2003). Organizing for resilience. In K. Cameron, J. Dutton, & R. Quinn (Eds.), *Positive organizational scholarship: Foundations of a new discipline.* San Francisco, CA: Berrett-Koehler Publishers, Inc, 94–110.

12 Weick, K., & Roberts, K. (1993). Collective mind in organizations: Heedful interrelating on flight decks. *Administrative Science Quarterly, 38*(3), 357–381.

13 Dougherty, D., & Takacs, C. (2004). Team play: Heedful interrelating as the boundary for innovation. *Long Range Planning, 37*(6), 569–590.

14 Hewitt, J., & Stokes, R. (1975). Disclaimers. *American Sociological Review, 40*(1), 1–11.

15 Lakoff, R. (1975). *Language and woman's place.* New York, NY: Harper and Row.

16 Linde, C. (1988). The quantitative study of communicative success: Politeness and accidents in aviation discourse. *Language in Society, 17*(3), 375–399.

17 Edmondson, A. (2003). *Psychological safety, trust, and learning in organizations: A group lens.* Cambridge, MA: Harvard Business School Press.

18 Edmondson, A. (1999). Psychological safety and learning behavior in work teams. *Administrative Science Quarterly, 44*(2), 350–383.

19 Kendra, J., & Wachtendorf, T. (2003). Elements of resilience after the World Trade Center disaster: Reconstituting New York City's emergency operations centre. *Disasters, 27*(1), 37–53.

20 Mallak, L. (1998). Measuring resilience in health care provider organizations. *Health Manpower Management, 24*(4), 148–152.

21 Edmondson, A., Bohmer, R., & Pisano, G. (2001). Disrupted routines: Team learning and new technology implementation in hospitals. *Administrative Science Quarterly, 46*(4), 685–716.

22 Kahn, W. (1990). Psychological conditions of personal engagement and disengagement. *Academy of Management Journal, 33*(4), 692–724.

23 Edmondson, A. (2012). *Teaming: How organizations learn, innovate, and compete in the knowledge economy.* San Francisco, CA: John Wiley & Sons.

24 Edmondson, A., & Nembhard, I. (2009). Product development and learning in project teams: The challenges are the benefits. *Journal of Product Innovation Management, 26*(2), 123–138.

4

PROVISIONAL LANGUAGE

Provisional ways of knowing

Innovation and entrepreneurship imply a kind of creativity. While many people tend to think of creativity as an individual ability, it frequently occurs in partnerships and teams. In fact, our cultural expectations about creators being single individuals might simply be a blind spot. Just think of Lennon and McCartney, Jobs and Woz, or even Jefferson and Adams for examples of creative pairs. Or think of the hundreds of people working together to create innovative technologies like the Mars rovers or state-of-the-art special effects for movies. More and more we are recognizing that complex acts of creativity are not the result of one person's big idea; they are the product of a team's coordinated ideas and efforts layered one atop the other over time.

Innovative entrepreneurship, of course, falls into the category of complex acts of creativity. So while we once thought of entrepreneurship as the quest of an exceptional individual, we now know that most successful ventures are started by teams. However, we also have come to know that in highly uncertain situations – such as the context in which entrepreneurs must work – few people or teams are at their creative best.[1,2] In fact, teams in unpredictable situations tend to experience diminished task-related agility, narrowed attention, and a diminished sense of team connectedness.[3,4,5]

Teams that can retain their creative capacity in the face of uncertainty tend to share certain traits. Chief among these traits might be the ability to notice new features and even subtle differences in their situation.[6] This capacity to notice is the foundation of what Ellen Langer at Harvard calls mindfulness.[7]

Mindfulness is a continual process of (re)drawing categories of distinction fueled by a willingness to accept new information.[8] Mindfulness theory posits that because uncertainty is constantly present – knowledge is always finite and circumstances are always changing – that team members should maintain a willingness to question things that they think they know. For example, most people would be quick to agree with the statement "One plus one is always two". But a mindful respondent would wonder under what circumstances might that statement not be true – and would realize that in some contexts, one plus one does not equal two. **(If you add one wad of gum to another wad of gum you get one really big wad of gum, not two!)**

It is easy to see how this kind of thinking could lead an entrepreneurial team to higher levels of creativity. Moreover, it is easy to adopt a mindful approach to entrepreneurial work. Doing so is as simple as noticing unexpected details that emerge, staying aware of multiple perspectives and contexts, and (re)framing observations with new categories of explanation when necessary. Several conversational features help successful teams maintain a mindful stance: frequent use of the conditional mood, the use of humor in team meetings, and an emphasis on spontaneity.

Conditional mood

Consider the difference between *is* and *could be*. When you frame things with the certainty of *is* – as in "this is a sofa" – you have categorized the item as one thing and one thing only. However, if you frame things with the flexibility of *could be* – as in "this could be a sofa" – you are free to associate this item with a variety of categories. It could be a sofa, but it also could serve as a bed, a fort in a child's game of pretend, or, regrettably, a cat's scratching post. By using could be instead of is, people tend to be able to experience higher levels of cognitive agility. They tend to be more creative.[9]

Sentences that use could or might in English are expressions of what grammarians call the conditional mood. For those readers who are a bit rusty on grammar, suffice it to say that English has three types of conditional sentences, but only one of them – the speculative type – evokes the conditional mood. It is a verb form that expresses a hypothetical variation on a given circumstance.[10] For example, the sentence "If I had done the demo, I could have started it with an explanation" showcases the expansive nature of the conditional, a mood that blends factual details of a situation with speculative possibilities regardless of the tense of the sentence's main verb.

The word *could*, of course, delivers the speculative meaning of the sentence in the most recent example. The verbs *could* along with *might* function to convey the concept of an array of options in any utterance. So, a speaker might say, "I could do the demo tonight", to indicate one possibility for the demo. (She is able to do the demo tonight or another time. Or, depending on the emphasis of the sentence, someone else could do the demo tonight.) Additionally, a speaker might say, "I might do the demo tonight", to express that she may do the demo tonight or another time.

In other words, the use of *could* or *might* signals the presence of multiple alternatives. Other words such as *probably* also imply a set of possibilities. The use of these words can help people to maintain an awareness of their imperfect and incomplete knowledge. The use of these words focuses people on searching for sound answers whereas more absolute language encourages people to search for *the* right answer.[11]

More resilient teams tend to use the conditional mood or other words that signal flexibility in their mind-set (e.g., probably) in their team meetings more frequently than low-performance teams. One way to understand this phenomenon is that because conditional framing permits an array of possible futures, it is the most accurate way for an innovative entrepreneurial team to speak about their work. People who recognize that complexities surround them are likely to perform better than those who deny or suppress the uncertainty, and the use of the conditional mood is an indicator of such awareness. Consequently, high-performance teams communicate their awareness of the dynamic and uncertain nature of their work through conditional language in their conversations with each other.

Let's see how TopCo's Sherri and Jack signal their awareness of uncertainty in this excerpt about plans to participate in a demo show.

Excerpt 4.1

Jack   So we're just going to go and have fun, learn about pitching, do the demo . . .

Sherri   People are probably going to ask some good questions. Answering them might get us warmed up for the pitch, might help us anticipate questions from the VCs.

Jack   Yep we'll need that energy boost; We're just going to fall asleep otherwise!

Sherri   Yep, totally.

Both   (laughter)

Sherri's use of the words *probably* and *might* signals her understanding of the unknowns facing TopCo at the event. Moreover, the imagined scenario she describes includes the possibility of input from unfamiliar others at the event, another dimension of unpredictability that is perceived in a positive way.

Jack's tongue-in-cheek reaction to Sherri's claim about using the questions as a warm-up suggests another means by which high-performance teams harness provisional ways of knowing: levity.

Levity

While the use of the conditional mood may be an obvious means by which high-performance teams signal flexible ways of knowing, it is not the only means. Levity also requires a capacity to hold multiple perspectives in mind. Humor paints a ridiculous portrait of a team's emerging situation – and it can be understood as ridiculous (and humorous) only if people can contrast it with a predicted and ordinary future scenario.

Levity can move a conversation to an imagined scenario that is disconnected from an expected future situation. When Jack suggests that they would fall asleep at the demo show without questions to keep them awake (in Excerpt 4.1), he is painting a possible future that crosses into the absurd. But because his suggestion is understood by Sherri to be playful, these statements that are disconnected from the team's real actions may actually enhance a team's focus and agility.

Levity also can help team members build thicker bonds with each other. Jack uses levity in this way in the following excerpt from one of TopCo's team meetings.

Excerpt 4.2

Jack	That's so your job around here.
Sherri	Right. (laughter)
Jack	Oh, I'll help out.
Sherri	Oh I know
Jack	(Pretending to hold a telephone) I'll be like will you please hold. I have to get Sherri.
Both	(laughter)
Sherri	okay . . .
Jack	Okay . . . I think that's a good thing for both of us to work on
Sherri	Yeah
Jack	I mean it's much more up your alley, but I think I can offer a view that's different than yours. Don't know if that will help . . .
Sherri	Totally, I agree this is something I need to focus on, but you need to think it through too.

When Jack jokes, "That's so your job around here . . ." and goes on to talk playfully about his lack of business savvy, he is saluting Sherri's expertise and their complementarity. And this is important to note: While high-performance teams are playful, they do not tease each other or make jokes at a team member's expense. Effective levity includes self-defacing humor that bonds people together.

Humor in all its constructive forms is an expression of play. Long associated with breakthrough ideas and innovations, play is an activity of choice rather than duty, set apart from the contexts, constraints, and consequences of regular activity and guided by its own structures and rules for participation.

Play seems to engender innovation because it transcends the boundaries of ordinary work.[12] When engaged in play, team members step into a temporary world that emphasizes exploration in the present rather than exploitation for future gain. It is a world that encourages experimentation. Whether those experimental ideas and artifacts materialize into meaningful contributions in the

context of a team's regular work does not matter; there are no negative consequences for unsuccessful attempts executed within the bounded world of play.
If, however, there is a seed of genius in the fruits of play it can be planted and
grown, so to speak, by the team in the real context of their work.

This connection between play and experiments can be seen clearly in the lean
startup approach to innovative entrepreneurship. Practitioners of lean startup
concepts hinge their success on deliberate experiments with prototypes en route
to defining their minimum viable products. Some might argue that the more
playfully teams can approach these experiments the more likely their success.
When their efforts are based in play, a lean startup team might be more agile,
better able to accept feedback or make changes in direction. Moreover, teams
that invite customers to play with their prototypes might get richer feedback that
can direct the development of their minimum viable products more effectively
than teams that use their prototypes as tools of persuasion.[13]

Acts of play are, by their nature, unpredictable and uncertain. Because failures
in the world of play present no adverse and lasting consequences, participants can
find pleasure in the uncertainty as circumstances unfold. They can tap into their
capacity to respond and react to the moment rather than plan and defend for a
serious future. In other words, they can relish the excitement that accompanies
spontaneous and improvisational interactions.

Spontaneity and improvisation

Often associated with music, improvisation requires the ability to listen and attune
to others, and to express yourself clearly. It also requires you to have deep knowledge (of your instrument and of music in general) and the ability to respond
instinctively and constructively in the moment.

Comedy also is associated with improvisation. According to acclaimed come-
dian Tina Fey, the four rules of improvisation are: agree with what has been
presented, build on what has been presented, offer constructive statements rather
than probing questions, and realize that there are no mistakes, only opportunities.[14] Fey's rules hinge on the idea that good improvisation is about accepting
the contributions that others have made and building on them rather than challenging them. In her respected view, improvisation is about being open to new
possibilities and continually moving forward in an affirmative and productive
manner no matter what unfolds.

Each of Fey's rules applies directly to the work of innovative entrepreneurial
teams in their quest to develop minimum viable products. Her third rule about
making statements is especially relevant. In her description, good improvisation
relies upon team members making statements that set a direction for everyone
else to follow, even if only for a very short while. This advice seems aligned
with the process of design thinking – an approach to innovation (made popular
by IDEO and, more recently, the Design School at Stanford) that connects the
development of product features arise, not with proposals about possible creations

but with assertions about the actual needs of potential (and specific) buyers. In other words, new product development tends to be driven by team members making informed and empathetic claims about people's expectations, frustrations, aspirations, and beliefs.[15] The existing design thinking research does not distinguish between the impact of conditional or absolute assertions. However, it does posit that product innovations emerge from statements about the defining characteristics of the market, statements that reflect the team members' diverse perspectives and knowledge.

An excerpt from TopCo's Jack and Sherri shows them building on each other's productive statements:

Excerpt 4.3

Sherri	Changing the size of the device is not really an issue
Jack	Well, within reason
Sherri	Sure, I mean at some size it becomes too big for the customer to carry around, but mechanically adding a foot is not any harder than adding an inch.
Jack	Right, You know . . . I think this section might be also a little bit too wide.
Sherri	Yeah
Jack	Because remember this adapter is going to stick out over here on the right
Sherri	Oh right.
Jack	Yeah so we need like a quarter inch or so of wiggle room on this side.
Sherri	And we don't have too much extra space going this way. Like even if we could redo this part to make it you know thinner . . .
Jack	Right
Sherri	Hmm . . . well we've got to get that part to fit on top . . .
Jack	What I could do is basically put this stuff on the back side . . .
Sherri	In that open area so that it
Both	becomes smaller
Jack	Yep
Sherri	Okay I'm good with that.
Jack	I'm on it.

In good improvisational form, each of them accepts the contribution that the other has made and adds to it. Utterance by utterance Jack and Sherri offer statements that present possible changes to their prototype. And even when they see that there is too little free space on the right side to follow their original design, they do not consider it to be a mistake, just an opportunity to tweak the design.

Moreover, the team begins by thinking about the user's experience. They empathize with the user who needs to carry this product with them. If the product is too heavy or unwieldy, customers will not be able to use it as Jack and Sherri hope that they will.

Fey's final rule of improvisation – that teams must keep moving forward and exploring new ideas – is critical for innovative entrepreneurial teams. Given the uncertainties of entrepreneurial work, teams will need to make changes to their products and strategies many times. However, teams that adhere to the guidelines of improvisation will not dwell on the past or place blame; they will look ahead and use what they now know to take a positive next step.

DO HIGH-PERFORMANCE INNOVATIVE ENTREPRENEURIAL TEAMS ASK A LOT OF QUESTIONS?

Conventional wisdom associates entrepreneurs with probing questions, and, for the past decade, entrepreneurship scholars and consultants have echoed that notion. Based on interviews with entrepreneurs, researchers have argued that highly successful entrepreneurs have a propensity to ask a lot of questions, especially questions that challenge the status quo.[16]

My research, however, takes a different approach. Instead of interviewing entrepreneurs after the fact, I study the observable language of entrepreneurial teams in action. Rather than rely on reports from entrepreneurs about their team interactions, I have teams record their team meetings, and I analyze the naturally occurring conversations that give rise to minimum viable products and successful new ventures.

My analysis contradicts conventional wisdom about questions (and specifically disruptive questions) and entrepreneurial success. In my research, the low-performance teams devote a slightly higher percentage of utterances to questions than the high-performance teams. And none of the questions posed by teams at either end of the performance spectrum attempts to buck the status quo. Rather, the teams in my research use questions to gather or clarify information or to seek opinions. They ask questions of each other in the service of comprehension, not disruption.

It is possible that disruptive questions might be asked in a different phase of the innovation cycle than I have studied. None of my data captured the teams' initial ideation conversations, for example; perhaps the status quo–challenging "what if" questions cited by other researchers occur primarily within that phase of the innovation process. It is also possible that the disruptive questions are asked of customers rather than teammates. It is easy, for example, to imagine "what if" questions being asked in the persuasive context of a sales meeting. Another possible explanation for the earlier results is that the entrepreneurs that were interviewed for those studies had been part of teams that maintained inquisitive cultures. A curious culture is not the same as a question-asking culture, but it is easy to imagine interviewees reporting the use of questions in their attempts to describe a culture of curiosity.

Less-advantageous ways of knowing

Not all teams are comfortable functioning in liminal states for a prolonged time. While high-performance teams benefit from provisional ways of knowing, low-performance teams rush into fixed, if false, ways of understanding the uncertainties that accompany entrepreneurial innovation. Low-performance teams tend to employ rigid and definitive forms of language, to impose false certainty on uncertain situations through the use of absolute claims and persuasion.

Absolute claims are used by speakers to present matters that seem certain and unchanging to them. Unlike conditional forms of language (such as *might* or *could*), absolute forms of language (such as *is* or *must*) convey a speaker's preexisting commitment to a particular interpretation. Moreover, one speaker's use of absolute language can inhibit other team members from offering alternative perspectives.

Persuasion is another conversational move that can limit interactions by influencing or devaluing a teammate's perspective. Like absolute claims, the use of persuasive language shows a lack of openness to new interpretations of the team's uncertain circumstances.

Both absolute language and persuasion can be found in this snippet from an UhOhCo team meeting.

Excerpt 4.4

Andy	Have you looked at what our competition is doing? Have you?
Bridgette	No.
Andy	Well what I've done is already better than their stuff. No doubt about it. If our product were available to buy today users would already get more bang for their buck than from anything else out there.
Carol	You know, I think that's true; like in terms of the spectrum of things the software does. But I don't think it's very easy to use. I mean that's what all of our interviews have said.
Andy	But there is a lot of functionality; a lot that users can do.
Carol	I think
Andy	(Cutting off Carol) So users have to upload some data to get the benefits. It's just a learning curve; users will enjoy knowing that they've personalized their experience after they get used to the way it works.

As is often the case, UhOhCo's conversation is colored by absolute and persuasive language when varied perspectives about the product emerge. Whether these alternative viewpoints offer subtle doubts or direct challenges, they are not allowed to be discussed at length. In this excerpt, Andy initially tries to impress upon his teammates that he knows best because he has examined a competitor's product more closely than they have. He eventually evokes absolute language to defend the product and the original vision for the product. He declares that his way of doing the work is the best and only way to proceed.

It is possible that users could see a product's bugs as features, a happy accident that most innovative entrepreneurial teams would be glad to accept. But when team members are trying to convince each other that the flaws pointed out by customers are actually desirable product attributes a happy outcome for the product seems unlikely.

What about brainstorming?

Provisional language allows teams to actively consider a wide array of possibilities. It also enables teams to construct new meanings from their discussion about these possibilities. Conventional wisdom might suggest that brainstorming accomplishes the same ends. However, provisional language is most helpful when it stays connected to the authentic features of a particular uncertain situation (such as customer feedback). In contrast, brainstorming sessions encourage and require contributions that are ungoverned by real market input.[17,18]

While brainstorming can be helpful to some teams, most innovative entrepreneurial teams do not have a shortage of imaginative ideas. Instead, innovative entrepreneurial teams tend to need help making sense of actual customer behavior. This problem can lead some innovative entrepreneurial teams to dismiss customer input (as in Excerpt 4.4) and use brainstorming as a kind of hedging technique.

For example, in a meeting in which the teammates of UhOhCo were discussing customer feedback, the conversation stalls as Andy expresses his frustration with customer concerns. He was receiving feedback that suggested the product needed to be easier to use and come with tutorials. He also heard that customers would be willing to pay a meaningful amount if the usability and tutorials met their expectations. Rather than explore how they could change the product to meet customer demands, Carol launches the team into a brainstorming session unrelated to the customer feedback or immediate next steps. After the brainstorm, Andy focuses on possible product enhancements for the distant future, and the team does not advance their product validation process at all. At no point did the team try to figure out changes that could be made to the product to meet the initial target market's demands.

A key to agility

Innovative entrepreneurial teams always need to be ready to pivot. Customer feedback can necessitate a change in the product. Competitive challenges can require a change to the strategy. **Because nothing is static or certain in entrepreneurial work, teams that embrace provisional ways of knowing may have an advantage. Teams that use the conditional mood, well-intended humor, and improvisational spontaneity in their meetings may have an easier time discarding old ideas and prototypes.** Provisional language allows teams to productively acknowledge and work with their lack of certainty. It also enables team members to hold multiple perspectives in mind. Building on this skill, reflective dialogue requires team-mates to consider and contrast different perspectives. The next chapter explores the importance of reflective language in the innovative entrepreneurial process.

Chapter takeaways

Provisional Conversational Competencies	What it is	Tips on how to cultivate
Conditional mood	Provisional verbs that include *would, could, might*	Reserve a level of commitment; retain flexibility and room for making changes.
Levity	Self-defacing humor, absurd portraits of future scenarios	Maintain playful stance; take your responsibilities seriously, but don't take yourself too seriously.
Improvisational skills	Spontaneous and positive comments and actions that build on recent contributions of teammates	Acknowledge, accept, and build on statements of others; avoid categorizing contributions as errors or missteps.

Questions for my team

How often do we use *would, could,* or *might*? Does one of us use these conditional verbs more than the other(s)?

What about humor? How often do we enjoy a good laugh in our work?

Do we constructively build on each other's statements? Or could our interactions include more gestures of acknowledgement and positive inquiry?

Notes

1 Amabile, T. M., Hadley, C. N., & Kramer, S. J. (2002). Creativity under the gun. *Harvard Business Review, 80*(8), 52–61.
2 Weick, K. E. (1993). The collapse of sensemaking in organizations: The Mann Gulch disaster. *Administrative Science Quarterly, 38*(4), 628–652.
3 Ibid.
4 Driskell, J. E., Salas, E., & Johnston, J. (1999). Does stress lead to a loss of team perspective? *Group Dynamics: Theory, Research, and Practice, 3*(4), 291–302.
5 Orasanu, J. (2005). Crew collaboration in space: A naturalistic decision making perspective. *Aviation, Space, and Environmental Medicine, 76*(6, Supplement), B154–B163.
6 Weick, K. E., Sutcliffe, K. M., & Obstfeld, D. (1999). Organizing for high reliability: Processes of collective mindfulness. In R. S. Sutton & B. M. Staw (Eds.), *Research in organizational behavior* (Vol. 1, pp. 81–123). Stanford, CA: JAI Press.
7 Langer, E. J. (1989a). *Mindfulness.* Reading, MA: Addison-Wesley Pub. Co.
8 Langer, E. J. (1989b). Minding matters: The consequences of mindlessness-mindfulness. In L. Berkowitz (Ed.), *Advances in experimental social psychology* (Vol. 22, pp. 137–173). San Diego, CA: Academic Press.

9 Langer, E. J. (1992). Matters of mind: Mindfulness/mindlessness in perspective. *Consciousness and Cognition, 1*(3), 289–305.

10 Mead, H., & Stevenson, J. (1996). *The essentials of grammar.* New York, NY: Berkley Books.

11 Badaracco, J. L. (2002). *Leading quietly: An unorthodox guide to doing the right thing.* Boston, MA: Harvard Business School Press.

12 Campbell, B. (2019). *Practice theory in action: Empirical studies of interaction in innovation and entrepreneurship.* New York, NY: Routledge.

13 Schrage, M. (1999). *Serious play: How the world's best companies simulate to innovate.* Cambridge, MA: Harvard Business Review Press.

14 Fey, T. (2011). *Bossypants.* New York, NY: Little, Brown and Co.

15 Matthews, B., & Heinemann, T. (2012). Analysing conversation: Studying design as social action. *Design Studies, 33*(6), 649–672.

16 Dyer, J. H., Gregersen, H. B., & Christensen, C. (2008). Entrepreneur behaviors, opportunity recognition, and the origins of innovative ventures. *Strategic Entrepreneurship Journal, 2*(4), 317–338.

17 Osborn, A. F. (1957). *Applied imagination: Principles and procedures of creative problem-solving.* New York, NY: Charles Scribner's Sons.

18 Perkins, D. N. (2000). *Archimedes' bathtub: The art and logic of breakthrough thinking.* New York, NY: W. W. Norton and Company.

5

REFLECTIVE LANGUAGE

Reflecting in action

Innovative entrepreneurial teams are supposed to be all about action. They are supposed to be comprised of supremely confident and decisive people who speed along to achieve a first-mover advantage. At least that's what the conventional wisdom would have us believe. But what if those stereotypes were misleading? What if successful innovative entrepreneurial teams were reflective teams as much as action teams?

Although not often called reflective practice, the behaviors that underlie the lean startup approach to developing a minimum viable project are, in fact, exercises in reflection. Between the stages of building product and measuring results of market experiments must be reflective dialogue about the data and the implications that the data might hold for the product or strategy.

Conversations to validate assumptions about a possible minimum viable product are essentially reflective dialogues between members of an innovative entrepreneurial team. They are verbal exchanges in which teammates assign and reassign meanings to their shared work by (re)considering the data they have, the assumptions they hold, and the next steps they could plausibly take.

Reflective dialogue leads a team to know its work differently – the advances in their work are the result of the new interpretations and meanings that they have developed through reflection.[1] Of course, there is a role in the entrepreneurial innovation process for conversations that lead to a team knowing more through the introduction of new, better, or different information. However, innovative entrepreneurial teams often have ample high-quality information. **Their success lies not in their ability to know *more* but in their ability to know *differently*.**[2]

While the term *reflective* might suggest that these dialogues are retrospective conversations about experiences long past, that is not necessarily so.[3] The process of reflection can be anticipatory, enabling active thought about possible alternatives and the likely result of possible actions.[4] Reflection also can occur in real time, enabling contemporaneous thought and action as an event unfolds.[5] In other words, teams can think about the consequences of actions before they take them, and they can think about something while doing it.[6]

In addition to the temporal aspects of reflection, reflective dialogue can focus on various levels of a team's experience. Teams can reflect on the content of their work (i.e., What are we doing?), the process of doing their work (i.e., How are we doing it?), and the premise for doing their work (i.e., Why are we doing it in this way, or why are we doing it at all?).[7]

Teams that are able to be reflective and proactive concurrently tend to do better than teams that are not. Similarly, teams that are able to reflect on various dimensions of their work are able to outperform those that are not. Two verbal moves, in particular, enable teams to sustain a productive reflective practice: reconsideration and suspension. These expressions of healthy self-doubt can protect teams from overconfidence and its negative consequences.

Reconsideration

Being able to hold multiple possibilities or perspectives in mind simultaneously is essential for reflective dialogue. To reflect, the members of an innovative entrepreneurial team must be willing and able to try on alternative ways of understanding what they are doing, how they are doing it, and why they are doing it. They must be willing and able to reconsider their assumptions and actions. Language forms that signal reflection – and especially reconsideration – are associated with high-performance innovative entrepreneurial teams.[8]

Reflective language is recognized by questions directed at the self: the individual or the team. It is language that demonstrates mental agility and situated humility. Verbal acts of reconsideration, in particular, reveal a team member's ability to introspectively review and revise meanings, to independently question their own assumptions and assessments without active prompting from someone else.

To illustrate a successful innovative entrepreneurial team expressing this kind of inward reassessment, let's check in again with Sherri and Jack, the co-founders of early-stage high-tech company TopCo as they prepare to demo their prototype to prospective investors.

Excerpt 5.1

Jack   You know that would be great, and that's actually what we should do, but we can't unless we get another engineer in the next ten minutes. So we can only really work on the slides, the pitch. Does that sound right?

Sherri   I guess that is right . . . So how can we . . .
Jack   Actually I'm not sure if we couldn't hack it in time for the meeting.
Sherri   You think?
Jack   Maybe we could just skip this bit, and have the users go from here to here? Kind of take out the glitch so no one fixates on that in the meeting and misses the stuff we want to showcase.
Sherri   That we can do. Awesome.

In this instance, Jack initially frames their situation as unchangeable; the problem with the demo is too great to remedy before the meeting. However, without any new information or perspectives coming from Sherri, he is able to conceptualize a way to improve the demo despite the limited time and technological assistance available to them.

Jack asks, "Does that sound right?" By posing that question to Sherri, he is seeking her critique of his assessment. As such, he is signaling healthy self-doubt, the recognition that he might be wrong about his initial assessment. What's more, asking the question aloud seems to stimulate his own review of his assessment – a review that leads him to revise the limitations he had falsely placed on the degrees of agency that the team actually had.

While this excerpt might make reconsideration look easy and automatic, it is rare for teams to be able to exercise this kind of productive self-doubt. All too often teams just accept their initial assessments of situations and push forward without reflecting. Instead of engaging in self-examination, many teams in TopCo's situation would simply work on the slides and finesse the story that they would tell to explain the demo's shortcomings.

At first, discovering that the language of self-doubt is associated with high-performance innovative entrepreneurial teams might seem surprising, but adaptive reframing has long been associated with group creativity.[9] Less-capable teams tend to demonstrate bravado rather than situated humility in circumstances that call for a reconsideration of what the team is doing, how they are doing it, and why they are doing it in that way.

Suspension

The essence of reflective practice is the ability to pause, however briefly, at critical instances to ask questions of the self or of the team. Sometimes the questioning occurs in real time as described in the section on reconsideration. However, sometimes the questioning is reserved for a future time.

When opting to suspend a conversation, a team demonstrates their ability to identify a matter that needs deeper consideration than they can afford in the present moment. Suspension also demonstrates a team's ability to hold a topic or course of action in an unresolved state without stopping progress along another dimension. Choosing to interrupt and return to a matter rather than dispense with it immediately requires an ability to function productively in the near term while keeping multiple possibilities open for the longer term.

It is worth noting that suspending a conversation is not the same as procrastinating or avoiding a conversation. To suspend a conversation is to commit to a future time to revisit and review circumstances, interpretations, and self-imposed limits. It is a thoughtful act that acknowledges the presence of an uncertainty so significant that it requires the team's focused and sustained attention. Sidestepping a difficult matter through procrastination or avoidance may look similar to suspension. However, such conversational dodges deny or suppress uncertainty while suspension productively grapples with it.

How does a successful innovative entrepreneurial team productively suspend their work? A snippet of a conversation between TopCo's Sherri and Jack provides a good example.

Excerpt 5.2

Jack	We've never been super confident about our numbers
Sherri	And we won't ever be. Like they're just models, best guesses. but I think adding this new variable will help.
Jack	Yeah, you know we should start fresh; try and ignore what we think we know right now . . .
Sherri	Yeah I totally agree.
Jack	Yeah okay that's what we'll do.
Sherri	But after tomorrow's meeting . . .
Jack	Yeah we need to set aside time for that, you know, deep dive . . . We'd show up tomorrow and be like "Um . . . we realized last night that this venture is not gonna work . . ."
Sherri	Unfurl the flag . . .
Both	(laughter)

By postponing an in-depth look at the financial projections, Jack and Sherri are temporarily holding on to the defining features of TopCo while acknowledging that the conversation that they are delaying might require them to abandon or adapt these features. They are agreeing to sustain a liminal state; to deliberately maintain a state of uncertainty about the ways in which the financials could impact the premise of their venture. Their actions are distinct from denial or avoidance – the team is aware of the uncertainties that await them in the review of the financials, and they are intent on grappling with them. But by choosing to suspend a confrontation with the financial data, they can attend to other pressing tasks and address these fundamental uncertainties later.

Suspensions are, by their nature, disruptions; a team is postponing a discussion or performative act until a future time. Suspensions force a team to hold some matters in a liminal state while continuing to make progress, however tentative those advances might be. Working in this realm of tentative progress requires discipline – to return to the topic later and to surrender any advances that have been made based on assumptions that do not hold up to the suspended review. Doing so requires some humility.

Situated humility and healthy self-doubt

To reconsider and suspend specific issues while moving forward requires team members to maintain a high level of situational awareness and self-awareness. They must be willing and able to question themselves and the assumptions that they hold. They must tap into their capacity for humility.

Seen as an important quality to be found in leaders and the corporate cultures they create, humility is considered to be especially valuable for organizations facing rapid and unpredictable change.[10,11] Even though changing conditions and uncertainty are inherent in the entrepreneurial experience,[12,13] humility is not frequently associated with entrepreneurs. Instead, entrepreneurs tend to be associated with confidence and sometimes overconfidence.[14,15,16]

An abundance of confidence may help entrepreneurs choose to start ventures and to persist in challenging situations.[17,18] However, there are limits to the positive impact high levels of confidence can bestow.[19,20] Consequently, top-performing entrepreneurs seem to be able to calibrate their confidence, to respond with lower and more appropriate levels of certainty when confronted with ambiguous or uncertain situations.[21]

This contextualized confidence, or "situated humility"[22] allows an otherwise confident entrepreneur to acknowledge his or her limitations in a given situation. It can be verbally expressed in a variety of ways, including the following:[23]

- Articulating a lack of knowledge or ability
- Admitting a mistaken action or assumption
- Praising others for their insights and contributions
- Seeking information and alternative impressions

Verbal expressions of humility can be especially valuable in the so-called pivot-or-persevere meetings that most startup teams eventually encounter. In the course of evaluating the validity of their product vision, teams occasionally must ask themselves if they are making real progress toward the creation of a viable venture. They must strive to identify faulty assumptions and revise their minimum viable product with the benefit of such insight.

It is easy to imagine how situated humility can help in a pivot-or-persevere meeting. Team members who are able to easily reveal mistaken assumptions and accept different interpretations, for example, will be much more agile. Rather than clinging to old notions that no longer adhere to the evidence as it is currently understood, team members will be able to adapt to new ways of conceptualizing the product.

Pivot-or-persevere conversations, of course, are meant to surface issues about discrepancies between the team's vision and the behaviors demonstrated by customers in a lean startup–style experiment. But they also can stir up issues about how the team members feel about changing the product and even about how the team members feel about themselves if the product and venture were to change. Team members with greater levels of situated humility will be able to productively align themselves with changes not only to the product but also to the venture and their own role in its success.

A glimpse into the unreflective practice of low-performance teams

Unlike high-performance teams that are able to reconsider assumptions and suspend decision making, low-performance teams are constrained by premature commitments and succumb to pressures to never look back.

Low-performance teams often resist making changes to their original product visions. On the plus side, vision statements can potentially help people imagine products before they exist. However, they also can pose a problem – vision statements can mimic certainty and diminish a team's pivoting ability. If team members ignore important evidence in order to stay true to the vision, they have lost the value of their lean-startup experiments.

Teams that are over-invested in their original vision statements might just keep developing the product and executing the plan as if they were doing performance art in a vacuum. Others – perhaps most – recognize that they are not making progress and attempt to find another market segment to love the product vision as is. This is the case of UhOhCo as this excerpt reveals.

Excerpt 5.3

Carol	I did some more interviews – that one with you and another one – and I've decided that working with this market niche is just too complicated . . . The better strategy must be to go more general. It's a bigger market – which is always good – and it'll be less complicated.
Andy	(Sigh) I did some more customer interviews, too. And it's like I keep having this same conversation over and over. Like, hello – I'm offering you exactly what you say you want. And after that interview yesterday that we did I was so frustrated because I'm like why is no one getting this? Why am I having this problem . . .
Bridgette	Yeah I'm with you. I went out and did another interview too. And so I'm telling this dentist about the product, and right away she's like, "oh, no . . . no one I know would use that in their practice". Blah blah blah. And like two minutes later she's telling me that her office like totally needs this, but she can't hear that that's what I've been saying. And I'm just like in my head like what's wrong with you? I'm like I just told you our product does all that, but she had made up her mind that the product wasn't relevant.
Andy	And I feel like – what am I not saying right that no one gets how revolutionary this is. What I've coded is already so much better than anything you can get today.

Carol   Totally

Andy   So I guess the general medical market is the better beachhead.

All the team members seem to recognize that their initial product idea is not getting traction. They come to that conclusion because the feedback that they have been getting is consistently at odds with the product vision. They seem to have little interest in developing a new vision to incorporate both the original concept and the guiding remarks from prospective customers. They seem irritated by, instead, of interested in the gap between the original vision and the market's reaction to it. Rather than taking time to consider a variety of ways to use the information from the interviews to alter their product vision, the team rushes to the conclusion that they must go after a different market segment (without any indication of interest from the "general" market). By suddenly changing their target market, they find a way to acknowledge the negative feedback without changing the product vision.

While this change of direction temporarily relieves some discomfort, it is not a productive pivot for UhOhCo. Had there been some indication of validation from a different market segment, they might have been justified in pivoting – but they did not have that. Low-performance teams like UhOhCo often fixate on the virtues of their vision as a technique for managing tension; the merits of the original product vision are contributed at moments when dissonance emerges between team members about the features of the prototype or when the feedback from the market is overwhelmingly negative. Had the team been able to reflect on their assumptions and choices in real time or in a future meeting they might have been able to use aspects of the feedback to direct constructive changes to their product or strategy.

As it was, UhOhCo could not find any uptake for their product in when it was presented to a less specialized market either. A few weeks later they returned to the original niche market as their beachhead even though they had gotten no validation from that segment. Once the team did not find any uptake for their existing prototype in the general market they simply chose to retreat to familiar, if unproductive, territory. Eventually they abandoned the product and venture entirely.

REFLECTING ON REFLECTIVE PRACTICE

Although many people have researched and written about reflective practice a significant amount of the credit for popularizing the concept goes to Don Schön.[24] His 1983 book, *The Reflective Practitioner*, has had an impact on many leaders from organizational consultants to community organizers – and now on innovative entrepreneurial teams. A major point of that book and later works by Schön was that organizational progress is achieved and sustained by the reflective and collective acts of team members. In other words, while trial and error might lead to lucky breakthroughs for an organization, continued success is more likely to come from a shared habit of learning through reflection.

In particular, Schön advocated mixing insights that can come from formal and informal ways of learning. For example, studying how to start a venture by taking courses, reading books, and adopting best practices will probably benefit an aspiring entrepreneur to some extent. However, there also is value in learning by doing, by starting a venture or interning in a very young company. And the real masters learn by integrating the lessons that emerge from both kinds of learning.

Reflection is a method by which individuals and organizations can synthesize various ways of knowing. It is also a process that can highlight differences between an organization's espoused theory and its theory-in-use: differences between what an organization says it believes in and what it actually does. By identifying and, if necessary, remedying the gap between beliefs and actions, teams can make their goals and actions more coherent. Moreover, having consistency between organizational value statements and task directives can lead to happier team members. If individuals can identify self-concordant goals that link personal purpose to organizational success, they are more likely to stay engaged with their work and to contribute to the organization for a long time.[25]

Schön, of course, did much of his work on reflective practice while he was a professor at Massachusetts Institute of Technology (MIT) between 1968 and his death in 1997. The Center for Reflective Community Practice and now the Co-Lab at MIT have continued to refine and apply his theory in a variety of contexts. In recent years, researchers there have articulated a method for reflecting on critical moments in a team's experience. This approach is designed to raise a team's awareness of the tacit learning that transpires in the course of doing their work. They have found that engaging in reflective practice empowers people to understand their work more completely and to build richer connections with co-workers and other stakeholders.[26]

Putting it all together

The goal of reflection is not to exploit knowledge or capitalize on unexpected events. Instead, reflection enables teams to (re)interpret what they think they know and to (re)interpret the meaning(s) of events that are happening (or have happened or might happen). Team-based reflection, of course, happens through dialogue. The conversational moves highlighted in this chapter – reconsideration, suspension, and situated humility – can help teams avoid overconfidence and pivot more productively.

This chapter and the two before it in this section have described the conversational competencies of innovative entrepreneurial teams. Your team's use of collaborative, provisional, and reflective language can play a role in your success. By using these conversational moves, your team can expand the interpretative exchanges that can lead to more successful pivots.

Fortunately, everyone can learn new language skills. The next section of this book highlights several exercises and practices that have been designed to help teams build awareness of language and incorporate more interpretive conversational moves into their work.

Chapter takeaways

Reflective Conversational Competencies	What it is	Tips on how to cultivate
Reconsideration	Introspective review and revision of meanings	Independently question one's own assumptions and assessments.
Suspension	Choosing to stop and return to a challenging topic	Point out the need to give the topic greater attention than the team currently can. Articulate when you will be able to productively return to the topic (e.g., a particular day or milestone).
Situated humility	Separating competence from overconfidence; maintaining a healthy sense of self-doubt and an awareness of the complexity of innovative entrepreneurial work	Say you don't know when you truly don't know; shift to a stance of curiosity.

Questions for my team

How often do we pause to reconsider what we think we know?

Have there been some instances when we proactively suspended a conversation and deliberately returned to it at a specific time?

Do we say "I don't know" when we don't know? Is one of us more likely to do that than the other(s)?

Notes

1 Kegan, R. (2000). What "form" transforms? A constructive-developmental approach to transformative learning. In J. Mezirow (Ed.), *Learning as transformation: Critical perspectives on a theory in progress* (pp. 35–70). San Francisco, CA: Jossey-Bass.
2 Heifetz, R. (1994). *Leadership without easy answers*. Cambridge, MA: Harvard University Press.

3 Raelin, J. (2001). Public reflection as the basis of learning. *Management Learning*, *32*(1), 11–30.

4 Scharmer, C. O. (2007). *Theory U. Leading from the future as it emerges: The social technology of presencing*. Cambridge, MA: Society for Organizational Learning.

5 Van Manen, M. (1995). On the epistemology of reflective practice. Teachers and Teaching: *Theory and Practice*, *1*(1), 33–50.

6 Schön, D. A. (1983). *The reflective practitioner: How professionals think in action*. New York, NY: Basic Books.

7 Mezirow, J. (2000). Learning to think like an adult: Core concepts of transformation theory. In J. Mezirow (Ed.), *Learning as transformation: Critical perspectives on at theory in progress* (pp. 3–33). San Francisco, CA: Jossey-Bass.

8 Campbell, B. (2019). *Practice theory in action: Empirical studies of interaction in innovation and entrepreneurship*. New York, NY: Routledge.

9 Hargadon, A. B., & Bechky, B. A. (2006). When collections of creatives become creative collectives: A field study of problem solving at work. *Organization Science*, *17*(4), 484–500.

10 Cameron, K. S., Dutton, J., & Quinn, R. E. (2003). *Positive organizational scholarship: Foundations of a new discipline*. Berrett- Koehler Publishers.

11 Weick, K. E. (1993). The collapse of sensemaking in organizations: The Mann Gulch disaster. *Administrative Science Quarterly*, *38*(4), 628–652.

12 Knight, F. (1921). *Risk, uncertainty and profit*. Boston, MA: Houghton Mifflin.

13 Ries, E. (2011). *The lean startup*. New York, NY: Crown Business.

14 Baum, J. R., & Locke, E. A. (2004). The relationship of entrepreneurial traits, skill, and motivation to subsequent venture growth. *Journal of Applied Psychology*, *89*(4), 587.

15 Hayward, M. L. A., Shepherd, D. A., & Griffin, D. (2006). A hubris theory of entrepreneurship. *Management Science*, *52*(2), 160–172.

16 Hmieleski, K. M., & Baron, R. A. (2008). When does entrepreneurial self-efficacy enhance versus reduce firm performance? *Strategic Entrepreneurship Journal*, *2*, 57–72.

17 Busenitz, L. W., & Barney, J. B. (1997). Differences between entrepreneurs and managers in large organizations: Biases and heuristics in strategic decision-making. *Journal of Business Venturing*, *12*(1), 9–30.

18 Hayward, M. L. A., Forster, W., Sarasvathy, S. D., & Fredrickson, B. (2010). Beyond hubris: How highly confident entrepreneurs rebound to venture again. *Journal of Business Venturing*, *25*(6), 569–578.

19 Hayward, M. L. A., Shepherd, D. A., & Griffin, D. (2006). A hubris theory of entrepreneurship. *Management Science*, *52*(2), 160–172.

20 Audia, P. G., Locke, E. A., & Smith, K. G. (2000). The paradox of success: An archival and laboratory study of strategic persistence following radical environmental change. *Academy of Management Journal*, *43*, 837–853.

21 Hmieleski, K. M., & Baron, R. A. (2008). When does entrepreneurial self-efficacy enhance versus reduce firm performance? *Strategic Entrepreneurship Journal*, *2*, 57–72.

22 Barton, M. A., & Sutcliffe, K. M. (2010). Learning when to stop momentum. MIT Sloan *Management Review*, *51*(3), 69–76.

23 Owens, B., Johnson, M., & Mitchell, T. R. (2013). Expressed humility in organizations: Implications for performance, teams, and leadership. *Organization Science*, *24*(5), 1517–1538.

24 Schön, D. A. (1983). *The reflective practitioner: How professionals think in action*. New York, NY: Basic Books.

25 Ben-Shahar, T. (2007). *Happier: Learn the secrets to daily joy and lasting fulfillment*. New York, NY: McGraw-Hill.

26 Amulya, J. (2004). *What is reflective practice*. Cambridge, MA: Center for Reflective Community Practice, Massachusetts Institute of Technology.

PART 3

Developing conversational competencies

Understanding the language forms that support high-performance is one thing. Incorporating them into your team's practice is another. This section offers some activities to embed in your meetings that can help your team develop and benefit from conversational competencies.

The next chapter presents several exercises that will help you in the same way that arpeggios and scales help an expert pianist. They are designed to strengthen your verbal capacity for agility and coordination – fundamental abilities that you will need to start and run a new venture. The chapter after that introduces the practice of documentation. Just as golfers can improve their game by filming and reviewing their swings, you will be able to gain valuable – and previously unrecognizable – insights about the process you are using to build your product and your venture by engaging in the practice of documentation.

6

EXERCISES TO BUILD VERBAL SKILLS

Building interpretive capacity

Innovative entrepreneurship is an interpretive act. The learning stage of the lean startup build–measure–learn cycle, for example, relies on teams making sense of the new information that they have gained from a customer experiment; it relies on a team's interpretive prowess. And, as the previous chapters have explained, there are conversational moves that can enhance a team's interpretive capacity.

The work of teams in other professional contexts – cockpits and operating rooms, to name a few – also is enhanced by specific verbal behaviors. Their work, however, is informed by immediate and clear feedback from planes and patients, and every flight and surgery concludes within hours. This is not the case for innovative entrepreneurial teams who grapple with highly interpretive and comparatively long feedback loops – even the most efficient lean-startup learning cycle is likely to take days. So while checklists and other tools have been developed to help cockpit crews and surgical teams succeed, different approaches have had to be crafted to help innovative entrepreneurial teams build the conversational competencies necessary for their success.

A promising way to improve your team's conversational competencies would be to start with a clear assessment of your current conversational practices. However, I doubt many readers will record, transcribe, and analyze the structure their team's interactions. Similarly, I doubt many readers could afford to have an outside consultant do a detailed verbal analysis of their team's meetings. Instead, I will suggest some more practical and applied activities that any innovative entrepreneurial team can use to enhance their conversational competencies.

This chapter starts with an overview of tips to help you develop collaborative, provisional, and reflective language skills. It then offers several exercises, or verbal routines that can help your team harness the power of the collaborative, provisional, and reflective (CPR) language forms in your work.

Basic techniques to foster collaborative language

A former colleague of mine, David Perkins, coined the phrase, "the lawnmower paradox".[1] The paradox is that it is much easier for a group of people to collaborate on the act of mowing a large lawn than it is for a group of people to collaborate on the act of designing a lawnmower. The design challenge is more difficult, in part, because it requires some technological know-how. However, even if the group were technologically astute, the design challenge would be more difficult because pooling mental effort requires interdependencies. Combining physical efforts to mow the lawn has much less complexity; all the group members can mow without any involvement with the other mowers.

Because a core task of innovative entrepreneurial teams *is* to design lawnmowers and other more complicated products and services, these teams must find ways to acknowledge and facilitate their interdependencies. They must develop ways of working – ways of talking – that enhance their capacity for collaboration.

While innovation and entrepreneurship are quite distinct from negotiation, these fields all emphasize the co-creation of mutually beneficial solutions – sometimes between people who hold divergent views on core issues. Because negotiation requires the creation and maintenance of strong relationships, some of the verbal approaches used by leading negotiators also can help teammates who have different views on their emerging product or strategy. Some examples of these conversational moves adapted for innovative entrepreneurial teams enacting a pivot include the following:[2]

- Help me better understand how you are making sense of the customer input we have. What do you think the customer feedback is telling us?
- Of all the things we've discussed in this pivot-or-persevere meeting what do you think is the most important?
- I'm worried about the pivot we're considering. Could you say more about your thoughts on the advantages (and risks) of pivoting in the way we've just outlined?

Each of these conversational moves embodies the core principles of collaborative language that were outlined earlier in this book. They tap into the power of the first-person plural. They heedfully seek feedback and share concerns. And they invite participation from all teammates on essential topics.

These conversational moves all express appreciation for the members of the team and respect different voices. As such they are likely to help teams surface the real issues that animate pivot-or-persevere decisions. They cannot, however, guarantee that teammates will agree on next steps, only that they can expose and explore the interpretations of data that will animate their pivot-or-persevere decisions. Provisional language can help them engage in productive play – and find clarity in possibly unexpected paths forward.

Simple practices to foster provisional language

While facilitating an executive event for Harvard's Learning Innovation Lab, I heard Ellen Langer recount a story that she has told in a variety of settings about horses and hot dogs. As I recall, she once was asked to watch someone's horse because the owner wanted to buy the horse a hot dog. In that moment she was incredulous; surely the owner knew that horses do not eat meat. The owner soon returned with a hot dog, and the horse ate it.

In my recollection of this story, it was told in that context to illustrate how easy it is to be mindless, to act as if we already know all of the possible interpretations of a given situation. Because she had been taught that horses, in general, were herbivores and her life's experience with horses had corroborated that view, she did not consider that this particular horse might like hot dogs. In other words, inflexible, absolute ways of knowing can give us a feeling of false certainty and lead us to incorrect conclusions.

Provisional ways of knowing, however, keep us focused on the present; what was true about the last horse I rode might not be true about the one I am riding right now, for example. When we operate from this more flexible, conditional stance we are better able to treat reasonable explanations as hypotheses that might be updated at any time rather than as unchanging facts. Provisional ways of operating demand that we retain a healthy skepticism about our explanations and continue to consider alternative interpretations rather than think we have got it all figured out.[3]

It may be uncomfortable for many people to endure the expanded uncertainty that a provisional stance requires.[4] However, some research suggests that highly successful organizations are guided by practices that do just that. Teams that anchor their actions on qualitative input from real customers in real time tend to do better than teams that are more reliant on models. Teams that deliberately construct meaning from unpredictable data from the market succeed because of their willingness to grapple with uncertainty. Teams that assume they can control or predict situations through the use of models or heuristics struggle to adapt to the uncertainties that they actually face and tend to perform poorly. The models give teams a false confidence which keeps them executing an unproductive or even destructive plan despite evidence from the market.

A simple routine that innovative entrepreneurial teams can use to maintain a provisional way of knowing is to evoke the conditional mood in their interactions. For example, by asking, "How else might we interpret this feedback?" you can invite productive conversation in pivot-or-persevere meetings.

By remembering to ask a question like this, team members can nudge themselves out of the false belief that their instinctive assessment is the only assessment. By including this kind of critical self-questioning in the process of pivoting, a team can better understand why they are making the choices that they are given the many uncertainties they face.

Provisional ways of knowing are supported by the use of humor and improvisation as well. Both of these aspects of healthy teamwork were featured in the executive event at Harvard in which Langer shared her horse and hot dog story. One of the signature exercises of the Learning Innovation Lab is a forum that allows one executive to present a real challenge from his or her workplace and collaboratively develop possible solutions with the group acting as if they were part of the presenter's team (not as external consultants). The means by which that group conversation is facilitated incorporates opportunities for improvisation and levity – expressions of collaborative language.

When participating in this exercise, group members are encouraged to offer their sincere suggestions of how the presenter might approach his/her problem. Unguided, the contributions might jump radically from one suggestion to the next, an experience that might leave the presenter without a chance to really internalize any of the suggestions. To give the presenter the best chance to really integrate the suggestions, a facilitator follows the first suggestion with a simple question: "Can anyone build on that?" This invitation allows other participants with similar suggestions to offer their contributions in a cluster. The cognitive task of the presenter is thereby streamlined; he or she only has to think about a single set of related suggestions initially. After a number of contributions along a similar line of thinking have been offered, the facilitator can then invite participants to start a different stream of contributions.

While the description of this group exercise may not sound like improvisation, it actually does follow Tina Fey's rules for improvisational work. Its structure requires participants to agree with and build on what has been presented. It invites participants to offer constructive statements and steers them away from asking questions of the presenter. And it withholds judgment about any of the suggestions, operating from a belief that there are no mistakes, only opportunities.

This group exercise also touches on levity. The facilitator sometimes evokes humor by asking, "What is the worst thing we [as a member of the presenter's team] could do in the situation s/he described?" In response to this question, participants are able to imagine and suggest absurd actions. Usually the responses generate laughter and build some comradery. Occasionally the responses contain a grain of a great idea that actually can be applied by the presenter. Either way, it tends to be a spirited, fun, and memorable exchange.

While lean startup teams are unlikely to have an external facilitator in attendance at their meetings there is no reason why a team member cannot ask transformational questions such as:

- How else might we interpret this feedback?
- Can anyone build on that suggestion?
- What about other options; can anyone offer contrasting suggestions?
- What is the worst thing that we could do in this situation?

By integrating these verbal practices into meetings, innovative entrepreneurial teams can leverage the conditionality, improvisation, and levity that are associated with high-performance. They can tap into the benefits that come from provisional ways of knowing.

Basic ways to foster reflective language

A few years back, Craig Newmark, the founder of the website Craigslist, was a keynote speaker at a public event related to the MIT $100K competition. Credited with revolutionizing the newspaper industry by his company's disruptive use of technology in the 1990s, Newmark said that the venture started as a hobby and that he had no ambitions of making such an impact. He also shared his recollections of two critical moments in the life of the venture: realizing that he was not the best person for the CEO role and selling a stake in the company to eBay (and not to other suitors that might have offered more dollars per share).

His descriptions of these two turning points revealed the reflective practice that he used as those events were unfolding. He described pausing to think and talk with his team about these pivot points. The decisions, he said, ultimately emerged from his sense of purpose about his work. To give power to a different leader whose talents would be better for the company's future and to forsake dollars per share to gain a partner that would be better aligned with the company's vision than other suitors were decisions that necessitated rich reflection on what the company could become. By revealing his situated understanding of these critical moments, Newmark demonstrated the importance of maintaining a high level of self-awareness and a willingness to question yourself and the assumptions that you hold (as well as the actions that may be culturally expected from you). His efforts to share his theories-in-use at critical moments – even if mitigated by the years that have passed since those experiences occurred – described the reflective practice that he relates to his success.

Newmark was able to ask himself and his team what felt right when faced with those two significant turning points. He was able to pause and reflect on core values that animated his life and the venture's direction. He was able to integrate those insights with data about the choices that faced the team. Then he was able to identify self-concordant solutions that moved the venture forward in a manner that was true to his and the organization's values.

In both cases he described, Newmark and his team knew that they were making decisions, and they reflected in advance of taking action. Other organizations, such as the U.S. military, rely on After Action Review (AAR) processes, a post facto evaluation of an event.[5] The AAR tends to be guided by questions such as:

- What was supposed to happen?
- What did happen?
- What are some improvements that we could enact next time?
- What should we try to do sustain next time?

A variation on this technique could be especially beneficial to innovative entrepreneurial teams. When looking back on a customer experiment, for example, a team might ask itself what about the event surprised them and what unexpected discoveries emerged from the event. This line of inquiry taps into a team's ability to identify and discuss what they still do not know or fully understand about their work. When followed up with expressions that demonstrate the capacity to suspend meaning-making – by asking when can we give this topic our full attention – teams promote the possibility of generating more accurate and actionable insights.

Importing other routines for effective discourse

A research initiative called Making Learning Visible has been a long-celebrated part of Harvard University Graduate School of Education's Project Zero, a research group dedicated to understanding the learning processes used by individuals and groups. The Making Learning Visible research makes recommendations for "thinking routines" that help individuals and groups understand the content of their work and learn from their observations and experiences.[5,6,7] The routines in their original form were developed with K–12 teachers and classroom learning in mind. However, adaptations of some of the routines can benefit innovative entrepreneurial teams engaged in lean-startup learning cycles.

Simply put, in a lean startup context, these routines are verbal activities that can help teams to understand why and how they are undertaking specific acts. They help team members consciously recognize the development of new insights – where the insights have come from, and what they might mean for the team's future. Many innovative entrepreneurial teams may lack awareness of the verbal practices that animate their work, but they probably have evolved some means to focus attention and facilitate meetings (including the all-important pivot-or-persevere meetings). Given that the chief task of an innovative entrepreneurial team is to learn from their iterative experiments, teams may benefit from routines that have been designed to promote the kinds of thinking and communicating that foster successful learning.

As innovative entrepreneurial teams navigate the lean-startup build–measure–learn cycle they are confronted with a need to evaluate customer data and update their ideas about prototypes accordingly. The learning (i.e., the new insights, explanations, and directions) that comes from these iterative practices might be improved by including variations of several routines in pivot-or-persevere meetings. Each of these routines will be explained in detail:

- Tell Me More – an exercise related to collaboration that surfaces interpretations and encourages different perspectives
- Reconsidering Beliefs – an exercise related to collaboration that stimulates additional inquiry

- Potentially Next – an exercise related to provisional framing
- Superhero Says – an exercise for levity and alternative framing
- Private Pivots – an exercise in individual and group reflection
- We Are Here – a critical review exercise to guide reflection on potential pivots and activate provisional ways of knowing

Tell Me More

This routine helps team members describe the meanings they have extracted from a customer experiment and asks them to explain their (possibly temporary) conclusions. It helps to anchor the team meeting in observations from the experiment, and it encourages team members to share diverse perspectives.

To enact this routine in a team meeting, a member of the team asks a core question, "Help me understand how you are thinking about this? What do you see (in our data, in our environment, etc.) that leads you to that conclusion?" The conversation that emerges can reveal the key aspects of the data that are shaping people's interpretations and explanations. Follow-on questions will be based on a particular context, of course. However, they may include inquiries that clarify a teammate's observations and prioritizations, inquiries that may begin with "Tell me more about" a particular matter.

It is important to remember that this exercise is about understanding. It is not about persuasion. Conversational contributions that start to argue for an alternative interpretation should be identified in real time and consciously suspended until another time. All teammates should be given an opportunity to share what they have noticed that has informed their interpretations before the team considers which observations and explanations to incorporate, at least for the moment.

Reconsidering Beliefs

This routine helps team members to integrate previous thoughts about the emerging product with new (and possibly unexpected) data from customer experiments. It helps teams to define the next build–measure–learn experiment to undertake.

Three questions form the heart of this routine:

- What do we believe we know now about the customer need?
- What puzzles us about the market needs (or about the product's features)?
- What actions can we take to clarify or resolve our puzzles?

To enact this routine, the team should allow everyone to respond to the beliefs and puzzles questions before opening up the conversation about potential actions. Listening to what people think they know and what questions they currently hold will guide the team members as they select future directions for exploration. Adhering to these phases ensures that all the team's ideas are available before they begin envisioning next steps.

As with the last routine, Reconsidering Beliefs is a context for appreciating the various viewpoints of the team's members. It works best when teammates bring sincere interest in each other's observations and ideas to the conversation.

If there are many puzzles to explore, part of the conversation about exploration will need to prioritize next steps. Constructive question prompts in such cases may include "What will we uncover if we explore a given puzzle in a particular way?" and "How will the investigation of a given puzzle impact our other puzzles?"

Potentially Next

This routine enables the team to consider possible ways to interpret information and envision pathways forward. It calls on each teammate to frame the team's current circumstances in a conditional and temporary way. It can help teams think differently about the information they have, the information they need to get, or the next steps that the team can take.

To enact this routine, one teammate puts an actual question facing the team in the center of the whiteboard. The question should be framed in the conditional. An example would be "What could be causing this unexpected customer behavior?" Another would be "How could we meet this new timeline?"

Circle the question and give each teammate a whiteboard pen. Individually, each team member draws at least one line out from the core question and writes a possible response. After everyone has exhausted his or her initial reactions to the question prompt, the team steps back to look at the whole. Questions can be asked to clarify particular responses, and duplicated responses can be consolidated. At that point, the teammates return to the whiteboard and add on to someone else's initial reactions. Each person draws a line from the first response and writes an action that would be possible or important to do if the first response were embraced by the team. Again, the team steps back to look at the full set of provisional trajectories. This time, the team can begin to discuss more desirable or feasible trajectories. (Until this phase, no assessments have been made, and fanciful or ridiculous trajectories are fine to develop.) As the exercise concludes the team can discuss common directions that emerged and outlier reactions that widened the field of possible next steps.

Superhero Says

This routine helps team members imagine alternative ways to interpret information and move forward. It allows each teammate to consider the team's current circumstances from the perspective of another person. It adds levity and helps the team think expansively about reasonable next steps.

To enact this routine, each teammate suggests a well-known individual to the group. Perhaps this person is a celebrated entrepreneur, but it could be a cultural leader in another domain (e.g., a president, artist, teacher, etc.) or a fictional character from a popular movie, book, television show, or comic strip. The names of these individuals are written on the whiteboard. For each suggested person, the team then answers the question, "How might _____ respond in our situation?" As teammates fill in the blank, some of the responses may be preposterous, and that is okay. The team should enjoy the levity. Sometimes silliness can spark a valuable insight. Other responses may have some recognizable gravitas that can prompt a conversation about a different way forward.

Private Pivots

This routine helps team members to engage in healthy introspection related to the team's work. It asks team members reflect on their thinking about the minimum viable product and to consider how, why, and when their thinking has changed. It can be useful in building team consensus when the product or the venture as a whole is going in unforeseen directions.

To enact this routine, all team members are asked to complete these two sentence stems:

* I used to think _____ about the definition of our minimum viable product (or our target market, end-user profile, etc.).
* But now I think _____ about the definition of our minimum viable product (or our target market, end-user profile, etc.).

It is important that all team members get to share their reactions to these prompts, and that the team members express appreciation for the variety of responses. And it can be helpful if the responses are placed on a whiteboard for teammates to see and compare.

Some teams may find it helpful to annex the Tell Me More routine after engaging in Private Pivots. By following "But now I think _____" statements with invitations to clarify, teams can hone in on the personal pivots individual team members have been making. Doing so can help teams diagnose why they may no longer have a singular vision for their venture – and may point them to new, more fruitful ways to conceptualize their work.

We Are Here

Using the points of a compass as a conversational guide, this routine helps team members to talk constructively about possible pivots. It helps team members consider various aspects of a proposed pivot prior to taking action.

To enact this routine several questions are asked, questions that begin with *N*, *S*, *E*, and *W*. Despite the contemporary convention of orienting with *N*, this exercise works best if teams begin with *E*, which stands for Excited. Teams then tend to progress to *W* (Worrisome), *N* (Need to know), and finally *S* (Suggestions for moving forward). The four key questions are

- E = Excited – What excites you about this proposed pivot? What is the likely upside if we do it as described?
- W = Worrisome – What do you find worrisome about this proposed pivot? What are the possible downsides if we do it as described? What is the most likely and what is the most worrisome outcome?
- N = Need to Know – What else do we need to know or understand to evaluate this proposed pivot? What additional information would help us to clarify whether we should undertake it?
- S = Suggestions for Moving Forward – What is your current stance or opinion on the proposed pivot? How might we move forward based on your evaluation of this proposed pivot?

It also is useful to ask team members to write down their initial judgments about the proposed pivot before doing the We Are Here exercise. Then afterward, ask them to consider how their thinking has changed based on the We Are Here discussion. (In other words, teams can evoke a variation on the Private Pivots routine to aid in constructive consensus building.)

Putting these routines to work

Just to clarify, no team should attempt to incorporate all these routines into every meeting. However, teams that can expand the interpretive dimension of their work by embedding collaborative, provisional, and reflective language into their meetings are likely to navigate pivots more successfully than those who do not. Perhaps some of these verbal routines will become standard parts of your pivot-or-persevere meetings. Perhaps others will be go-to exercises in circumstances that are especially challenging for your team to resolve. Or perhaps you will adapt one of these routines to suit the unique needs and style of your team and its meetings. The important thing is to find ways to expand your team's interpretive conversations.

All of these verbal exercises can be made visible; they can be documented in a visual way that can be the source of future conversation and learning for your team. The next chapter delves more deeply into the practice of shared documentation.

Chapter takeaways

Way to expand interpretation	Prompts to start conversations	Routines to enact
Fostering collaboration language	"Help me better understand how you make sense of the customer input we have". "Of all the things we've discussed in this pivot-or-persevere meeting what do you think is the most important?" "I'm worried about this one aspect of the pivot we've proposed. What do you see as some of the advantages (and risks) of pivoting in the way we've just outlined?"	Tell Me More Reconsidering Beliefs
Fostering provisional language	"How else might we interpret this feedback?" "Can anyone build on that?" "What is the worst thing we could do in this situation?" "How might __ respond if he or she were in our situation?"	Potentially Next Superhero Says
Fostering reflective language	"What about the data/the experiment surprised us? What unexpected discoveries have we made?" "How does this proposed pivot fit with our values as individuals and as a company?" "When can we give this issue our full attention?"	Private Pivots We Are Here

Questions for my team

Which language form – collaborative, provisional, or reflective – feels the most natural or habitual for me in my workplace conversations?

Which one feels the most unusual to me?

When can our team try each routine to expand our use of interpretive language?

Notes

1 Perkins, D. N. (2000). *Archimedes' bathtub: The art and logic of breakthrough thinking*. New York, NY: W. W. Norton and Company.
2 Fisher, R., & Shapiro, D. (2005). *Beyond reason*. New York, NY: Viking Adult.
3 Cadsby, T. (2011, July 25). Why being certain means being wrong. *Harvard Business Review*.
4 Michel, A., & Wortham, S. (2009). *Bullish on uncertainty: How organizational cultures transform participants*. New York, NY: Cambridge University Press.

5 Morrison, J., & Meliza, L. (1999). *Foundations of the after action review process* (Special Report 42). Alexandria, VA: United States Army Research Institute for the Behavioral and Social Sciences.
6 Rinaldi, C., & Gardner, H. (2001). *Making learning visible.* Cambridge, MA: Harvard University Press.
7 Ritchhart, R., Church, M., & Morrison, K. (2011). *Making thinking visible: How to promote engagement, understanding, and independence for all learners.* San Francisco, CA: Jossey-Bass.

7

MAKING INTERPRETATION VISIBLE THROUGH DOCUMENTATION

Externalizing the process of innovative entrepreneurial work

Innovative entrepreneurship is a complex social phenomenon.[1,2] Companies and products develop through the interactions that people have with each other. Ideas about products, for example, are strengthened, reshaped, and replaced when they are externalized through speaking, writing, drawing, and prototyping. In fact, making prototypes is a very powerful way of externalizing ideas and refining them based on the social interactions that they inspire. This is why crafting minimum viable products through the build–measure–learn cycle is the focus of lean startup teams.

Of course, the meta-task of innovative entrepreneurial teams is to learn how to be better innovative entrepreneurial teams; to learn about and continually develop their practice. Just as product-oriented learning is improved by making a team's work visible through prototypes, practice-oriented learning is improved by making the way a team works visible, too. By finding ways to see a model of how their innovative entrepreneurial team does its work, team members can improve the means by which they accomplish their shared goals.

Some of the routines mentioned in the last chapter readily lend themselves to visualization. For example, the We Are Here routine is easy to depict graphically: write $E–W–N–S$ on a whiteboard, and allow team members to write their responses to the $E–W–N–S$ question prompts in the appropriate quadrants. Then the team members can step back and collectively examine their individual impressions. Perhaps they can see that what excites (E) one teammate worries (W) two others, for example. Or perhaps by seeing the sheer number of things people think that they need to know (N) before pivoting in a proposed direction reopens a conversation about the best next step for the team. The point is that seeing helps many people think.[3] Plus, seeing can stimulate new and necessary conversations and actions that lead to better innovations and organizations.[4]

Making the lean-startup learning cycle visible is valuable for precisely these same reasons. By externalizing the process, teams can discover the drivers that animate their actions, and with that awareness they can coherently review and revise their actions. Moreover, the visible documentation of the learning cycle allows teams to undertake a retrospective view of a series of pivots over time. This ability is especially valuable if a team starts to feel like it has been going around in circles instead of pivoting productively. And making the cycle visible delivers at least one other benefit: It ensures that all team members feel heard by recording their contributions in plain sight.

Defining documentation

If the phrase "making interpretation visible" sounds strange or intimidating at first, you can relax. You only need to master a few basic concepts and import them into your team meetings, especially your pivot-or-persevere meetings.

The first thing to realize is that documentation is not decoration. Visually recording your team's workplace practices is not about the creation of beautiful images or clever cartoons. Nor is it about the rendering of infographics. Productive documentation, of course, can be artful, but the goal is not aesthetic integrity; the goal is purposeful utility. This means that the style and appearance of your team's documentation are less important than how (and how consistently) your team captures the content of its workplace interactions.

It also is important to understand that documenting your team's interpretive practices is not the same as making agendas or keeping minutes from meetings. Productive documentation captures the *dynamism* of your team's interactions and decisions as they take shape. It reveals how your team comes to make choices about changes to the product or strategy. In other words, while agendas and minutes capture a record of *what* your team did in its meetings, documentation in this sense captures *how* your team goes about doing its shared work in its meetings. **Making interpretation visible means documenting the way(s) your team makes sense of key events, puzzles, ideas, and acts.** It means documenting the way your team engages in the innovation process that propels your product and venture forward.

The most important concept to grasp, however, is that the artifacts that you create through the documentation process are your tools. They are material resources that can inform conversations about your team's ongoing approach to innovative entrepreneurship. They both reveal your interpretive practices and enhance your evolving capacity for interpretation. The combination of the documentation process and the conversations that the resulting artifacts inspire can help your team understand how you do your work – and how you can do it better.

The what and how of documentation

When applied in a lean startup context, documentation focuses team attention on the stages and outcomes of the build–measure–learn cycle in order to enhance a team's capacity for innovation. It transforms the resources, assumptions, and other elements of the innovation process into visible artifacts. **Just as proto-typing makes your team's ideas about a product visible in a material form,**[5] **documentation makes visible your team's interpretations about the product – what it could be, how you can create it, and why you are creating that specific product in that specific way.** It produces a material artifact of the invisible process of reasoning that gives rise to the practical accomplishment of your team's shared work.

While you can productively document almost any team interaction, capturing pivotal moments in your team's work may be highly beneficial. Consequently, the following description focuses on the documentation of a pivot-or-persevere meeting. But no matter what experience you choose to document, making your team's interpretive process visible includes:

- An opportunity for all team members to notate their perspectives on key aspects of the innovation process
- An invitation for all team members to discuss the artifact that has emerged from that shared activity of notation
- An act to capture and save the artifact for the team's future reference (either as a photograph or in the whole form of the original object)

Enacting the three steps

The key topics that form the structure for this exercise can emerge organically. However, pivot-or-persevere meetings are occasions when a team really needs to understand its interpretive processes, and such meetings tend to develop around a set of predictable topics. These topics provide the scaffolding for the notation.

For example, in a pivot-or-persevere meeting, a team's current prototype tends to be described with an emphasis on any specific features that were tested recently by customers. New data that has come from customers, advisors, and relevant others tends to dominate the meeting. The current assets that the team has – the tangible and intangible resources that can be applied to learn more about the minimum viable product – also tend to come up. And proposed pivots are likely to emerge near the end of the meeting.

The ultimate vision for the company may or may not be articulated explicitly in every pivot-or-persevere meeting. And while it changes over time for many teams, the vision presumably has been the focus of earlier meetings and may not be revisited each time. Similarly, the team's intended product definition and market definition may have been hashed out earlier. Consequently, like the overall vision, these magnets for the team's attention and aspiration do change from time to time, but they may or may not be actively considered in a given meeting. However, the current vision and the current intended product and market definitions are part of the shared understanding of the team, and they do orient the team's conversations.

Often unspoken but ever present are the assumptions that each team member uses to interpret data and recommend future actions. These assumptions are the beliefs about the limitations of agency, customer interest, and other matters that have not come from direct observations of customer behavior. They are, in essence, a team's interpretation engine.

Because they are rarely verbalized, assumptions usually remain unrecorded and unexamined. Moreover, assumptions are almost never visibly externalized. Without visual cues it may be difficult for teams to recognize the assumptions that are leading them astray in their attempts to develop their minimum viable products. The lack of visible cues also may make it difficult for teams to discuss the impact that assumptions – especially faulty assumptions – are having on their work as innovative entrepreneurs. Moreover, the lack of a record of assumptions over time may make it very difficult for teams to find and critique patterns in their process.

To the extent that teams visually produce anything in their pivot-or-persevere meetings, it is usually one person at a whiteboard writing key words (often nouns) that he or she wants to emphasize. The writing on the board often represents one person's impression of what he or she imagines that everyone thinks and often is done to recap problems or to advocate for a particular solution. Sometimes, a teammate will sketch of a prototype on a whiteboard (or digital tablet or even a napkin). Again, this visual representation is often done to frame the current product situation or to propose a particular product change. While these ways of notating a meeting can be useful, they are not the only ways – and they may not be the most beneficial ways.

Step 1: using scaffolding to invite notation

Documentation essentially starts with a pressing question. In the case of pivot-or-persevere meetings, the question is obvious: Should we pivot (and, if so, in what way), or should we continue on our current path? In other circumstances, of course, the guiding question will differ.

Next you will need some scaffolding to structure the documentation process. This can be accomplished by writing several key topic areas across the top of a whiteboard: current prototype, assets, new information, proposed pivot(s), assumptions, revised proposal(s), product and market intention, and intended outcome. If you do not have access to a whiteboard you can write those column headings on sticky notes and affix them to any vertical surface.

Under each heading, all team members should contribute sticky notes with relevant information and impressions. While different colored sticky notes (or pens) for different topics are visually helpful they are not essential; one color can also work.

This is the essence of the first step of the documentation process. It is a fairly intuitive act, but teams that adhere to some basic guidelines may get the most out of the activity:

- Make sure everyone on the team participates.
- Allow a short period (not more than 5 minutes) for this first step.

Step 2: starting a constructive dialogue about the emerging document

Once all team members have been able to add as many sticky notes as they feel necessary in every category, the team can step back and have a look. This marks the beginning of the second phase of the documentation process – an invitation to discuss the document.

The conversation might start by consolidating similar sticky notes. If two people have posted essentially the same piece of customer feedback under New Information, for example, the team can talk about that and remove duplicate notes. If two people, however, have posted contrasting notes then the conversation needs to focus on understanding these different impressions of their shared experiences.

The notes associated with the category of Assumptions are likely to require the greatest amount of conversation. Assumptions are rarely discussed overtly, and team members may be surprised at the array of impressions that people have formed. By exposing and examining the underlying assumptions that are animating the team's work, the conversation may point to potential pivots that had not yet been considered.

During the conversation, sticky notes may be temporarily (and then permanently) revised or replaced. This is a chance to work in a liminal space, to talk about what it might mean to change any of the pieces of the team's current plan. It is a time when new insights and big ideas can advance a team's thinking about the content, process, and premise of its shared work.

Eventually the team will settle on the sticky notes that best represent the team's current understanding of their work. Those notes become the final document for the session.

Again, this step in the process of making a team's interpretive processes visible is best accomplished by following a few guidelines:

- All contributed notes are received with respect and appreciative curiosity.
- Everyone on the team is actively encouraged to participate in the conversation.
- A longer period (not more than 30 minutes) is devoted to this step.

Step 3: capturing the document for future use

Once the conversation has run its course and the document has come to its final configuration for the day, it is time for the third step of the documentation process. One of the team members needs to photograph the whiteboard and its contents. Alternatively, someone could transpose the contents of the board into

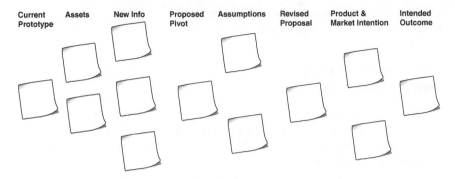

FIGURE 7.1 Documenting the interpretation process on a whiteboard

another format (e.g., writing notes in a notebook or keeping the actual sticky notes). The important thing is to capture and keep the visualized documentation of the team's interpretive work. The team can use this record in a reflective mode in the future to compare the interpretive processes used in a series of their meetings over time.

The guidelines for this third step are straightforward:

- Save the file in a manner that lets you read the contents of the document.
- Attach the date of the meeting to the file in some manner.

There is more to be said about the documentation process. But before we expand on the existing descriptions, let's consider how a specific team might engage in the documentation process.

A scenario of a founding team engaged in this exercise

Imagine, for example, if the struggling UhOhCo had used this technique in their pivot-or-persevere meetings. Andy, Bridgette, and Carol would have posted sticky notes in the various categories. Based on excerpts from the conversations described in earlier chapters, their sticky notes might have included the following points:

- Prototype – medical records software
- Assets – $1,000, free office space, extensive and knowledgeable network
- New information – ease of use is an issue, people don't see a need for the product
- Proposed pivot – change from dental offices to a more general medical market segment

- Current product intention – build a high-quality cutting-edge software product
- Current market intention – dental offices (initially – a change proposed right now)
- Current intended outcome – venture-backed software company, high-growth high-tech company, top-tier partners

The task of identifying and writing down their assumptions, however, might have been more difficult. Perhaps someone would have been able to recognize that the team was committed to finding a customer base for the product as it was originally conceptualized and that they assumed a customer would want the product exactly as they have envisioned it. At a minimum, perhaps someone would be able to identify that they were proud of their product as it is and that they were interested in building a company that was known for cutting-edge technology. Sticky notes would then be added in the assumption category about their beliefs:

- Assumptions – our product is the best on market already; cutting-edge technology is our strategic advantage; pivoting on the market front is better/easier than the product front because the product is so revolutionary

Once the UhOhCo team members could see such notes about their assumptions they would have a much easier time questioning them. They would be able to talk about their beliefs and the impact of those beliefs on the team's agility. Perhaps they could ask each other what would happen if they were willing to make changes to the product rather than switching market segments.

A team at this point in the exercise is typically able to recollect other pieces of feedback from customers and add more sticky notes to the category of New Information. In the case of UhOhCo, the team members might be able to add notes with specific feedback they had gotten about ease-of-use problems. Alternatively, perhaps they would be able to add notes with data from customers about changes that they would have liked (i.e., instead of simply noting that there were ease-of-use issues they could specifically name the design or functionality suggestions that customers had made).

After engaging in this discussion and reworking the necessary sticky notes the team may have a better pivot to propose. But even if they decide that the first pivot proposal is the best one they will have a more coherent understanding of why that is the choice they are making. They will be able to move forward as a team with a deep appreciation for the work they are doing, why they are doing it, and how they are doing it.

At a future time, if the team needs to revisit its pivots, the artifact generated by the documentation process can help the team recollect the means by which they selected the pivot that they did. Consequently, the final step in the documentation process is to capture the documentation. One of the team members can take a digital photo and save it, taking care to note the date of the meeting in the image or in the file name. Alternatively, someone can keep the artifact itself for future reference.

The power of documentation increases over time

All too often, lean startup teams find themselves stymied by the pivoting process. They try to the best of their abilities to engage in the learning cycles and other features of the lean startup methodology, but, like UhOhCo, they find themselves going in circles. When this happens tempers can flare, people can give up, and teams can self-destruct.

Teams that make interpretation visible can use the saved artifacts from earlier documented meetings to avoid or get out of this rut. The saved documents are data points that reveal your team's interpretation processes over time. By comparing the documentation from each of your pivot-or-persevere meetings, you will be able to identify patterns in your team's approach to developing a minimum viable product. That data and the insights that spring from this meta-analytical exercise will enable your team to work more effectively and pivot more productively.

The process for the retrospective meta-analysis of saved documentation is similar to that which guided the creation of the initial documents. The only additional step comes at the beginning:

- An opportunity for all team members to view the saved images
- An opportunity for all team members to notate their observations about the set of documents
- An invitation for all team members to discuss the new artifact that has emerged from this shared notation
- An act to save the new artifact for future reference

The guidelines, too, are similar to the set associated with the initial documentation process. They again hinge on full participation conducted in a spirit of respectful and appreciative inquiry and occurring within agreed-on time limits.

There are differences, however, between the two exercises. In the initial exercise, the point is to document the interpretive process being used to navigate a specific pivot (or to stay the course). In the retrospective meta-analysis, the point is to uncover the enduring dynamics that have shaped a series of pivots. These habits of the team's interpretive processes might be helping or hindering the team's productivity. Consequently, understanding what these processes are and how they are influencing the team's work is important. To focus the conversation on the team's habitual patterns of interpretation, the categories for notation and discussion might include: Consistencies repeated across most meetings,

Constantly changing aspects of our work, and Flip-flops (going back and forth between two pivot points).

Once the team has explored the similarities and differences in their observations about the set of documents, they can conclude this exercise by capturing an image of the meta-documentation for future reference.

How documentation helps develop conversational competencies

Using collaborative, provisional, and reflexive language helps teams accomplish the act of documenting their interpretive processes. And the reverse is true as well; the act of making interpretation visible helps teams exercise these core conversational competencies.

The documentation process evokes the interpretive language forms through the activity of making the artifact. It is collaborative and invites equal participation: Making the artifact involves everyone working on the same thing at the same time. It is provisional: The sticky notes are temporary representations of the team's information, meanings, and actions as they are understood in that moment. It is reflective: The exercise asks team members to recollect features of their shared work and to (re)consider the meanings of their data points and the directions they suggest.

Doing the documentation exercise also invites team members to use collaborative, provisional, and reflective language while they create the artifact. As team members put up sticky notes and look at them, they spontaneously tend to seek clarification and share concerns. These collaborative conversational moves are used when team members ask why certain assumptions are being made and why certain pivots are being proposed, for example. The documentation process also prompts teams to use provisional conversational moves. As they see each other's impressions and assertions, they often reach for hypothetical ways of exploring the pivot, riffing on the possibility that a different scenario could unfold. Sometimes the hypothetical explorations include levity and absurd possibilities. Humorous exchanges about the worst pivot the team could make, for example, are often a part of the documentation activity. Teams also tend to find themselves relying on reflective conversational moves during the documentation process. As they pause to think about the story the sticky notes are telling about their venture they are engaging in reflection. Such a moment often inspires reconsideration. Teammates also have an opportunity to express situated humility by articulating limited knowledge, admitting mistakes, and praising each other for insightful contributions during the activity.

In short, the documentation process supports a team's development of conversational competencies because it is a forum for noticing and listening. It provides an explicit opportunity for teams to describe the interpretive work that they have been doing – and to engage in an interpretive conversation about that record of their work. In other words, the process of making interpretation visible is an exercise in mindfulness.

Why making interpretation visible helps teams pivot

As described near the start of this book, mindfulness is a practice of actively noticing new or disruptive data while maintaining awareness of multiple perspectives and possibilities.[6,7] It is widely believed to be an asset to teams functioning in uncertain contexts such as entrepreneurship, conferring on them advantages of creativity and agility.[8,9] And, when teams are pivoting, anything that can help them be more creative and more agile is a boon.

In addition to helping teams tap into their creativity and agility, documenting the interpretive process can give teams a boost of positive energy. Doing the documentation exercise feels good to innovative entrepreneurial teams because it is a shared activity with immediate and tangible output. It is a rare occasion when everyone on the team is doing the exact same thing, the entire project is completed within the hour, and the team has a physical artifact to show for its effort. This experience of a successfully completed task sometimes can help people feel more encouraged about the demanding work that they must do collectively, yet individually, over a longer time – especially if the current pivot requires the team to let go of a cherished part of the previous vision.

The documentation process is a context for psychologically safe engagement.[10] The mediated nature of the exercise encourages more participation and less defensiveness than other ways that teams might conduct a pivot-or-persevere meeting. For some people – especially teammates of very strong lead entrepreneurs – it is easier to critique the document or a specific sticky note than it is to challenge a particular person directly. The documentation process creates a nonthreatening forum for rich conversation. If the exercise gets more teammates talking more frankly (albeit politely) about the future of the team's product and venture, then better pivots are likely to result.

In the process of documenting their build–measure–learn cycles teams are able to access the thinking of the whole team. It allows them to ask questions of clarification and offer alternative suggestions to enhance the team's meaning-making abilities and enhance their productive pivoting abilities.

Moreover, the benefits of documentation increase over time. The artifacts that the team creates in each pivot-or-persevere meeting provides a record of how their understanding of their shared work has evolved. Looking at the collection of artifacts as a whole facilitates individual and team thinking about pivotal moments in their venture and about the means by which they habitually do their shared work.

There are many benefits to be had from the process of making interpretation visible – and there are many ways that teams use documentation exercises in the development of their products and ventures. The next section of this book explores some of the ways that innovative entrepreneurial teams have incorporated the practice of making interpretation visible into their work.

Chapter takeaways

Feature of the documentation process	Why it matters	Tips
Visually capture key events, puzzles, ideas, and acts that propel your innovation and venture forward	It is a forum for noticing and listening; for considering the nature of the interpretive work that you have been doing in order to pivot productively	Documentation is not a decoration, agenda, or meeting minutes; it does not need to be pretty.
Steps include 1) Notation, 2) Disucssion, and 3) Capture of the artifact	Each step is an opportunity to understand how your team is interpreting its context – and to recognize new (and better) options that you might have missed	Strive for equal participation; make sure you understand each other's notations.
Topics to document can include: - Current prototype - Assets - New information - Proposed pivot(s) - Product and Market intentions - Intended outcome	Visually representing each category helps teams hone in on assumptions that can shape particular pivots and long-term outcomes	Sticky notes may be combined, revised, or replaced during the conversation.
Retrospective meta-analysis referring to the artifact	It is a means to uncover the enduring dynamics that have shaped your team's pivots over time. New categories might include: - Consistencies repeated across most meetings - Constantly changing aspects - Flip-flops	Use a digital camera to capture your documentation Routinely make time to talk about how you tend to enact pivots (i.e., Do you always change markets instead of changing the product?).

Questions for my team

What have we captured (in written or other visual form) from our past pivot-or-persevere meetings?

What do we usually write on the whiteboard during our pivot-or-persevere meetings, and how is that different from the documentation process?

What do we usually write on the board in other important meetings, and how is that different from the documentation process?

MAKING INTERPRETATION VISIBLE

This documentation exercise helps teams interpret the uncertainties that influence their product development and market strategy. It is conducted within pivot-or-persevere meetings, but it can be useful in nearly every team meeting.

Documentation starts with a pressing question. From that point, the three-step process helps teams to build connections – between data points and with each other's perspectives. It also encourages the use of collaborative, provisional, and reflective conversational moves.

To document your work you will need sticky notes (ideally in at least six different colors), markers, a writing surface (ideally a whiteboard), and a digital camera.

Step	Activities and tips
1) Notation	Categories can be developed organically, but the following categories tend to facilitate most pivot-or-persevere meetings: - Current prototype - Revised proposal(s) - Product and market intentions - Current intended outcome The categories are written in column form on a writing surface such as a whiteboard. All team members write relevant information on sticky notes related to each category. The notes are placed under the proper category for all to see.
2) Discussion	This step starts as team members act to consolidate similar sticky notes. Team members then talk about contrasting notes and explore the different impressions people have about the work. Significant time should be allowed to discuss the category of Assumptions. Once the underlying assumptions that animate the team's work are exposed, team members should reconsider possible pivots. During the conversation, sticky notes should be revised or replaced to represent the emerging ideas. The conversation concludes with an articulation of next steps. Whether teams have opted to pivot (in a new way or in an already-articulated way) or persevere, the team members will have a richer understanding of why they have come to this conclusion.

As you wrap up, pause to reflect on the exercise itself; express what was helpful or confusing about the activity and its end state. Thank everyone for contributing ideas and for being supportive.

3) Capture   A team member should take a digital photo and save it, taking care to note the date of the meeting in the image or in the file name. The image will be used in a future meta-analysis of the team's interpretive processes. (If no camera is available, a team member can keep the artifact as a whole by affixing the columns of sticky notes to a large piece of paper.)

RETROSPECTIVE META-ANALYSIS

This exercise is used after several pivot-or-persevere decisions have been made with the aforementioned documentation exercise.

It helps teams examine the assumptions and practices that characteristically shape their work.

The process enables team members to identify the habitual approaches that the team uses to conduct its work and to question whether those are the only or best ways.

To engage in this exercise, you will need the images from previous documentation exercises, sticky notes, markers, a writing surface (ideally a whiteboard), and a digital camera.

Step	Activities and tips
1) Examination	Make the previously captured images available for all to see. Each person should look for patterns in the documents (i.e., Do we always change the market and never the product when pivoting?). This step can be done in advance of a meeting by team members individually. Or it can occur in a shared time and space.
2) Notation	Categories can be developed organically, but the following categories facilitate most retroactive assessments: - Consistencies repeated across most meetings - Constantly changing aspects of our work - Flip-flops

(Continued)

(Continued)

Step	Activities and tips
	These categories are written in column form on a writing surface such as a whiteboard.
	All team members write relevant information on sticky notes based on their observations from the examination step. The notes are placed under the proper category for all to see.
3) Discussion	Start by identifying similar sticky notes. Talk about dynamics that more than one person has noticed. Also talk about any contrasting notes and explore the different impressions people have about the same phenomenon. Consider whether any habitual practices are really helping the team meet its goals. Open the conversation to explore ways that the team might avoid some dynamics and expand others in the future.
	During the conversation sticky notes should be revised or replaced to represent the emerging ideas.
	Take time to reflect on the exercise itself as you wrap up; share what was helpful or confusing about the activity and its end state.
	Thank everyone for contributing ideas and for being supportive.
4) Capture	Take a digital photo and save it, taking care to note the date of the meeting in the image or in the file name. The image can be used in a future meta-analysis of the team's interpretive processes. (If no camera is available, a team member can keep the artifact as a whole by affixing the columns of sticky notes to a large piece of paper.)

Notes

1 Dimov, D. (2007). Beyond the single-person, single-insight attribution in understanding entrepreneurial opportunities. *Entrepreneurship Theory and Practice, 31*(5), 713–731.
2 Gaddefors, J., & Anderson, A. R. (2017). Entrepreneurship and context: When entrepreneurship is greater than entrepreneurs. *International Journal of Entrepreneurial Behavior and Research, 23*(2), 267–278.
3 Comi, A., & Whyte, J. (2017). Future making and visual artefacts: An ethnographic study of a design project. *Organization Studies, 39*(8), 1055–1083.
4 Suchman, L. (1995). Making work visible. *Communications of the ACM, 38*(9), 56–64.
5 Suchman, L., Trigg, R., & Blomberg, J. (2002). Working artefacts: Ethnomethods of the prototype. *The British Journal of Sociology, 53*(2), 163–179.
6 Langer, E. J. (1989). *Mindfulness.* Reading, MA: Addison-Wesley Pub. Co.
7 Langer, E. J. (1997). *The power of mindful learning.* Reading, MA: Addison-Wesley.

8 Krieger, J. L. (2005). Shared mindfulness in cockpit crisis situations: An exploratory analysis. *Journal of Business Communication*, *42*(2), 135–167.
9 Wilson, D. (2007). Team learning in action. *Doctoral Dissertation*, Harvard Graduate School of Education, Cambridge, MA.
10 Edmondson, A. C. (1999). Psychological safety and learning behavior in work teams. *Administrative Science Quarterly*, *44*(2), 350–383.

PART 4

Using interpretive language in various situations

Using collaborative, provisional, and reflective language helps innovative entrepreneurial teams pivot productively. In addition, these conversational competencies enable teams to handle all sorts of other challenges. This section explores an array of dilemmas that innovative entrepreneurial teams tend to face, and the ways that language and documentation exercises can help teams thrive.

8

INTERPRETIVE LANGUAGE AND A TEAM'S FINAL PIVOT

All good things . . .

There are many different types of pivots.[1] Some involve changes to the product. Some involve changes to the market segment. Still others involve changes to a business model or other strategic matter. None of those pivots are inherently good or bad, pleasant or unpleasant. However, one type of pivot is dreaded by almost every founding team: The need to assess whether a company should be shut down.

Not everything works. Even the best, most agile team can come to a point at which the best thing to do is to close down the venture. For example, in the months after 9/11 numerous young ventures shut down. The world around them had changed radically; funding was scarce, and buying centers became more conservative in their pacing and their purchases. Even ventures that had seemed viable and full of realistic potential on September 10 of that year suddenly faced the need to abort.

There are, of course, better and worse ways of shutting down a company. The optimal ways of disposing of assets, handling customer relationships, and officially disbanding the team and closing the company as a legal entity are skills that need to be learned. Fortunately, good advice on the mechanics of shutting down a venture is widely available from government websites, popular magazines, textbooks, and the wider entrepreneurial community.[2,3,4,5]

Shutting down a venture is a process and not an event. And almost always, that process begins with a sensitive conversation between the members of the founding team. **Collaborative, provisional, and reflective language can help teams successfully shut a venture down as well as start one up.**

Portrait of a final pivot

Early on things looked bright for Bea and George. She was an experienced marketing person with a good track record in emerging new media companies, and he was a superstar engineer with significant experience in young technology ventures. From their previous work experiences, they knew a lot about how consumers used the web and how scalable web infrastructure needed to be designed and built. As they talked about their experiences and interests, they began to develop a vision for a collection of websites. Eventually they decided to work together to make their vision happen.

Their initial vision was to make a coordinated series of websites for individuals navigating major inflection points over the life span: graduation, marriage, divorce, retirement, and so on. Their thinking was that people at those stages needed predictable types of information, wanted to talk with other people going through the same transition, wanted to have access to experts in predictable topic areas, and needed to make predictable purchases in a limited timeframe.

Bea quit her job and worked on the venture full-time; George kept his day job and contributed to the venture in the evenings and on the weekends. In their earlier conversations, they had already done storyboards for the sites and had outlined the technological features that the initial version of the sites would require. So their first real shared goal as a team was to mock up a site. She did the design work and the HTML, and he knit together the infrastructure to enable the content, commerce, and communications functionalities.

With this prototype at the ready, the team was able to raise $50,000 in a friends-and-family round. This enabled them to do some lean-startup style tests and to hire some outside help to make some of the necessary adaptations and improvements.

According to Bea, their early conversations were more about how to get everything done and less about what to do. While they had customer interest and participation on the site, they were uncertain about how to make a business out of these positive indicators. So they talked with cautious optimism as they made plans, set goals, and made adjustments along the way.

Many of their early meetings were filled with updates; they had to inform each other of progress and problems with the interdependent development paths they were on. But the updates were not only about the exchange of information. They were also a means of engaging each other's opinions about the unfamiliar parts of the business.

Despite their deep knowledge in their respective areas, neither of them had been a founder before, and neither had ever done sales. So while they had confidence in the interface, infrastructure, and audiences for the sites they were developing, they were less sure about how to sell advertising (which was their initial business model). Consequently, a large part of their team meetings was spent on how to package the ad space, how to meaningfully measure its effectiveness, and how to test their hypotheses about their business model.

The first prototype site included content and peer-communications capabilities; the commerce functionality would wait until the basic appeal of the site was verified. With this early version of the first site live, the reaction from end users was overwhelmingly positive. Users were eagerly consuming the content and conversing with each other; each day the measured behavior was improving in terms of the number of users and time on the site per user.

This good news was easy for Bea and George to talk about in their meetings. Secure that they were on the right track, they could focus their team meetings on how to monetize the cultural success of their fledgling site.

Bea started to line up meetings with potential customers – now as sales calls rather than as discovery sessions. However, despite their enthusiasm for the site, prospective customers were not being transitioned into active customers; they were not ready to buy advertising. Reflecting on the unsuccessful sales calls, she recognized that prospective customers were interested not in advertising to their user groups but in learning about them. It seemed like there might be interest for customized market research based on the qualified user groups that she and George were aggregating on their site.

With that new piece of information, the focus of their team meetings changed. Suddenly Bea and George were discussing changes to make to the backend technology to accommodate research methods such as surveys and diary panels. They were considering how to package and price market research instead of ads. They were meeting with new prospective customers from a new market segment. They were reaching out to new advisors. And they were discussing how to incentivize users to participate in research requests. However, the *way* they were talking didn't change much; they were still heedfully seeking each other's impressions and ideas.

Nevertheless, the team's progress stalled. Tensions began to rise. Something was wrong and had to be addressed.

By deconstructing the pivot that altered their business model from advertising to market research, Bea and George were able to identify the problem. When they made their interpretative process visible, they could see that they had different expectations and levels of commitment. Bea had the assumption that George would focus full-time on the venture now that they had validated the concept and were ready to respond to real customer interest. George, however, had no such intention; he had no plan to quit his existing job to pursue what to him was a hobby. George held the assumption that Bea would use this as a platform to build a small consulting business and was surprised that she was really committed to building a high-growth company.

Bea and George used documentation to examine their pivot and their present dilemma. With their new understanding of their situation, Bea and George realized that they were facing a very different pivot: Should they split up and/ or change the team, or should they dissolve the company. Using their conversational competencies, especially those related to provisional ways of knowing, they were able to productively discuss an array of options and possible outcomes. Shortly thereafter, for a variety of reasons that were meaningful to them, Bea and George opted to dissolve the company.

While this might not sound like an entrepreneurial success story, I would argue that it is. Even though Bea and George had uncovered what looked like a real opportunity, it was not an opportunity for them at that time. Without wasting additional time, money, or social capital, Bea and George were able to amicably shut down the company, learn from it, and move on. Bea was able to use this experience to become a successful intrapreneur in the next chapter of her career, and George was able to achieve significant intrinsic and extrinsic rewards for his work as an engineer and inventor. This makes their final pivot and their entrepreneurial journey, as a whole, a success.

Bea and George were able to fail forward, to learn from a failed entrepreneurial effort and take a constructive step forward into new personal and professional identities. **I like to call founders who can do this *toasted marshmallows*: They are slightly burned by their entrepreneurial experience but profoundly improved by it.**

THE DOCUMENTATION PROCESS FOR A FINAL PIVOT

If your team has come to the point of discussing whether or not you should shut down the venture, you need to attend to this topic with care. If you have been in the habit of documenting your pivot-or-persevere meetings, you may find that the artifacts can help you identify patterns of decision making or enduring assumptions that have contributed to your current dilemma. With that awareness your team can consider an array of next steps – including the end of the venture.

If you have not made your interpretation process visible in past meetings, then this would be a time to start. Documentation begins with a pressing question such as "Is closing the venture our best move?" You will need the usual materials (sticky notes, pens, a whiteboard, and a digital camera). You may write the usual categories horizontally across the whiteboard, but a variation can be helpful when considering the closure of a venture (Current prototype, Assets, New information, Proposed pivot [i.e., closing the venture], Assumptions, Revised proposal[s], Most recent product and market intention, and Most recent intended outcome).

The first step, the notation process, begins once everyone is assembled. Everyone writes relevant information on sticky notes and places them under the proper category for all to see. For example, Bea and George's whiteboard included the following notes when they began the second step, the discussion:

- Prototype – market research backend system/behavioral and relational buying patterns
- Assets – about $12,000 in the bank, great advisors with links to venture capital, good relationships with lead customers
- New information – one key team member is not going to work on the project full-time (ever), but he can work a few hours per week long-term

on a casual basis; one prospective customer has signed a nonbinding letter of intent
- Proposed pivot – change the team or shut down the company
- Assumptions – we need a full-time chief technology officer (CTO); our technology is our competitive edge; without a crackerjack full-time CTO we cannot define or deliver the offering
- Most recent product intention – breakthrough software that easily interfaces with legacy systems used by our beachhead market to understand buying patterns
- Most recent market intention – luxury department stores; luxury shopping district associations
- Most recent intended outcome – venture-backed company (exit to be determined)

As the discussion unfolds, allow time to probe the assumptions. You should revise, replace, or remove sticky notes as you explore clarify or expand on the concepts. When you are ready to articulate a next step for the team, you are ready to finish the discussion step. Take time to thank everyone for engaging in the process.

The third step is simple: Capture an image of the whiteboard in its final state.

The language of resilience

Once a team decides that the venture has reached the point of no return, they still have a lot to do. With fresh uncertainties, big emotions, and limited time, the stakes might seem as if they have never been higher. Consequently, how team members talk with each other during the process of shutting down a company matters. Skillful conversations can make the experience productive, empowering team members to learn not only about business but about themselves. Teams with underdeveloped conversational competencies, however, might come away from the experience worse for the wear.

While contemporary culture is very forgiving of entrepreneurs who try and fail, we probably all know at least one entrepreneur who did not bounce back quickly after shutting down a young company. For example, I can think of a person whose despair over his failed venture lingered for a very long time, costing him a dear relationship and perhaps much more. Being able to separate his failure in business from his identity as a person seemed to be difficult for him. Only after finding some purpose in the entrepreneurial phase of his life was he able to move on with his professional and personal life.

Finding purpose in failure is an attitude frequently found in resilient people and teams. The values that guide individuals and organizations play a big role in a person's or team's ability to withstand adversity, including the failure of a venture. Two other traits of resilient people and teams are their ability to cope with – rather than hide from – reality and their ability to use whatever resources are available to improve their circumstances.[6]

Resilience also has a linguistic dimension. If your team can use collaborative, provisional, and reflective language while shutting down the company, you might become toasted marshmallows. In other words, how your team talks can influence your ability to take the failure of the venture in stride.

The language of resilience has four primary features: heedfulness, improvisation, healthy self-doubt, and shared modes of expression.[7] Each of these features, in fact, has been described in earlier chapters because they relate to the language forms associated with high-performance teams. Heedful interactions are collaborative in nature. They include an individual's ability to empathize with and anticipate the needs of the team as a whole; to subordinate one's individual orientation to the service of the team. Improvisational exchanges exercise provisional language. People who are skilled at improvisation have procedural and declarative knowledge about the task at hand that they can use in creative ways, and their creativity is enhanced by seeking help, giving help, and framing their claims with conditional language.[8,9] Healthy self-doubt hinges on a capacity to reflect. Checking assumptions, questioning what you think you know, and admitting errors could express the cautious wisdom related to resilience. Shared modes of expression rely on a team having a singular understanding of risks, goals, and possible actions; as such, they are expressions of collaboration. Teams that participate in conversations equally and have overlapping conversational roles (e.g., everyone shares in the responsibility of facilitating team meetings) tend to be more resilient.

All the interpretive language moves that are associated with high performance apply to the act of successfully ending a venture. Given that teammates must continue to work together, teams can find value in the use of the first-person plural, for example. The use of conditional verbs such as might and the ability to reconsider assumptions can help teams avoid making premature cognitive commitments to dead ends while steering toward an exit. And the use of humor can help teams tame the stress that can accompany the final stages of a venture's existence.

It seems easy and obvious: If collaborative, provisional, and reflective language can help teams achieve better outcomes then the same conversational competencies should help them reach the best possible exit. Yet, as intuitive as it seems, some teams still struggle to maintain a flexible stance and use interpretive language as the venture reaches its end stage.

New types of uncertainty are in abundance as various exit scenarios are explored, and teams often lose some agility in such unpredictable and stressful situations. In this crucible, the aforementioned misperceptions about innovative entrepreneurs – the need to be, or at least to look, bold, passionate, and fast – can disrupt a team's interpretive ways of communicating and derail their efforts to use a lean approach to finding the best ending.

Just as teams that are building a venture benefit from using interpretive language to grapple productively with uncertainty so do teams that are closing a venture.

After the venture is done

Many serial entrepreneurs will tell you that it is possible to learn from failed ventures, and they are right.[10,11] It is also possible to learn nothing from the experience. The difference between the two outcomes often lies in reflective practice.

In the weeks and months immediately following a failure, you might need to grieve your loss.[12] That is understandable. Everyone needs time to process the emotions that emerge when a venture is finally over.

Not all of the work of grieving is somber. Some teams, for example, have a funeral or a wake for their venture.[13] They invite friends and colleagues who were familiar with the venture, present eulogies to celebrate the life of the venture, and say good-bye to the venture in a playful way.

Recently I have been encouraging teams to use games to help them cope with a failed (or failing) venture. But regardless of the way that you process your grief, any raw emotions you feel eventually should give way to more thoughtful contemplation about what happened, when, and why. When it does, you may find reflective dialogue can help you and your teammates articulate the lessons that you have gained from the experience.

Simply put, a failed innovative entrepreneurial venture will leave you with stories and contacts by default, but acquiring insights from the experience requires effort.

Sometimes exits are a happy achievement!

Of course, while most ventures will not make it, some do! Even the most successful ventures will have to have an exit strategy. And teams that are able to navigate successful exits will rely on their conversational competencies.

While an initial public offering (IPO) often is heralded as the ultimate outcome, many innovative entrepreneurial teams opt for acquisitions. Being acquired is another process with another learning curve, and founders who intend to take this route need to prepare their skills.

In the early phases of exploring possible acquisition teams may have a discovery session with a potential suitor. In these meetings, participants from both companies exchange information on the market, their products, their core talents, and their aspirations. If a reasonable fit seems possible, the representatives from both companies continue the exploration with more emphasis on details – including sensitive issues such as financial matters.

These inter-team conversations are distinct from the intra-team conversations that have dominated your team's work until this point. They are not performances; you are not overly selling the other team on your company. However, they are more formal – and more sensitive – than the backstage, private interactions you have with your own team. Nevertheless, the same core conversational competencies will serve you well.

Collaborative, provisional, and reflective language can help you frame and execute an acquisition. Collaborative language enables you to forge a bond with your potential acquirer. By referring to your two teams together as *we* you help the other company's personnel envision a shared identity and a seamless workflow. Similarly, by demonstrating heedfulness in your interactions, you will convey the sense that you are attuned to the needs of the collective enterprise. Provisional language also facilitates healthy acquisitions. By using *could* and *might* in the inter-team meetings you prevent premature commitments and prompt expansive consideration of different deals. And reflective language moves such as reconsideration and suspension allow everyone to navigate the decisions and advance transitional plans thoughtfully.

Many ways to learn

Whether your company closes on a high or low note, it is an occasion for learning. By enacting the work of being an entrepreneur, you and all of your teammates have learned something about entrepreneurship. But the question remains: What have you learned?

Experiential learning is a valuable part of an entrepreneur's education, of course, but it is only part of the learning process. In addition to the enactment phase of learning, the reflective processes of selection and retention help entrepreneurs to develop their abilities.[14] After engaging in an entrepreneurial venture, entrepreneurs naturally reflect on their experience and, consciously or not, they decide which parts of that experience were formative. They select which specific experiences taught them about entrepreneurship and what those critical lessons were. Eventually, entrepreneurs apply those self-discovered lessons in future endeavors; they embrace certain lessons, retain them, and use them in future endeavors.

If your venture has failed, conversations between teammates and with advisors who knew the failed venture can help entrepreneurs find the lessons that were embedded in their shared experience. Inspired by the military After Action Review process, you could directly ask each other questions such as:[15]

- What went well?
- What could have gone better?
- What should we do differently or try to repeat in future endeavors?

Or you could play a game that I call *Toasted Marshmallow*. Sometimes serious and sometimes silly, the game's question cards prompt conversations that help team members process their feelings, contextualize their experiences, and reimagine their professional identities. The game uses question and activity cards to guide teammates through conversations about the meaning of the venture to each of them on personal and professional levels. As the game progresses, teammates can give each other appreciation chips to acknowledge especially insightful or courageous responses. Winning occurs by having the most chips at the end of the game. (More about the *Toasted Marshmallow* game can be found in the Appendix of this book including a do-it-yourself kit of game cards.)

If your venture has had a happier exit, conversations between teammates and with advisors are still important. It is in these transitional interactions that you can take stock of the lessons learned during the course of a particular venture. These interactions also are where you start to envision your next chapter as an individual. As you think about the people and organizations that have been helpful to you, you may begin to consider the ways you can contribute to the entrepreneurial ecosystem, possibly as an advisor or investor. Alternatively, you may realize that you are excited to start all over again with a new venture at your earliest opportunity to do so.

While the *Toasted Marshmallow* game is especially beneficial to teams who are facing failure, the game can be useful to teams going through an acquisition as well. Both outcomes in the life of a venture are personal and professional inflection points, and the game gives teammates a way to structure conversation about the transitions.

Ventures end for many reasons. Conversations always play a role in the decision to sell or shut down a venture, and the way that you talk about a final pivot matters. This chapter has presented several suggestions that can help you and your team talk productively about the possibility of closing your venture. Of course, founding teams face many other challenges that must be addressed through conversation. The next chapter touches on the ways that collaborative, provisional, and reflective language can help you navigate some of the most frequently encountered dilemmas of early-stage innovative entrepreneurial teams.

Chapter takeaways

Common issues related to a final pivot	Productive approaches	Tips on how to enact
Evaluating radical changes (e.g., founder exits, dissolving the company)	Avoid premature cognitive commitments and give yourself time to consider an array of possibilities.	Use provisional language to discuss various options and possible outcomes.
Managing the stress related to ending the venture (or achieving another exit)	Keep the workplace interactions positive.	Use levity; include good-natured humor in your team's interactions.

(Continued)

(Continued)

Common issues related to a final pivot	Productive approaches	Tips on how to enact
Continuing to work together productively while experiencing intra-team tension	Remember that you are a team and that people are doing their best in an imperfect situation.	Use first-person plurals, heedfulness, and humility in your interactions.
Wanting to fail forward	Take time to talk about the venture and make sense of your experiences with your teammates.	Play the *Toasted Marshmallow* game with your teammates; cultivate resilience through your conversational moves.

Questions for my team

How are we talking when we talk about the possibility of shutting down the venture? (Variation: How are we talking when we talk about the possibility of an acquisition or other exit?)

What processes have we put in place to manage the emotions, stress, and other challenges that have arisen in this stage of the venture's life?

What can we do to mark this transition and make it as constructive as possible for the whole team?

Notes

1 Ries, E. (2011). *The lean startup*. New York, NY: Crown Business.
2 Belicove, M. (2012). How to properly close your business. *Entrepreneur*. Retrieved April 30, 2018 from https://www.entrepreneur.com/article/224113
3 Gov.UK. (2018). *Selling your business and closing down*. Retrieved May 2, 2018 from www.gov.uk/browse/business/selling-closing
4 Hisrich, R. (2014). *Advanced introduction to entrepreneurship*. Northampton, MA: Edward Elgar Publishing.
5 SBA. (2018). *Close or sell your business*. Retrieved from www.sba.gov/business-guide/manage-your-business/close-or-sell-your-business
6 Coutu, D. L. (2003). Sense and reliability: A conversation with celebrated psychologist Karl E. Weick. *Harvard Business Review, 81*, 84–90.
7 Weick, K. E. (1993). The collapse of sensemaking in organizations: The Mann Gulch disaster. *Administrative Science Quarterly, 38*(4), 628–652.
8 Hargadon, A. B., & Bechky, B. A. (2006). When collections of creatives become creative collectives: A field study of problem solving at work. *Organization Science, 17*(4), 484–500.
9 Moorman, C., & Miner, A. S. (1998). The convergence of planning and execution: Improvisation in new product development. *Journal of Marketing, 61*, 1–20.
10 Danner, J., & Coopersmith, M. (2015). *The other "F" word: How smart leaders, teams, and entrepreneurs put failure to work*. Hoboken, NJ: John Wiley and Sons.

11 Shepherd, D. A., Williams, T., Wolfe, M., & Patzelt, H. (2016). *Learning from entrepreneurial failure*. Cambridge: Cambridge University Press.

12 Shepherd, D. A. (2003). Learning from business failure: Propositions of grief recovery for the self-employed. *Academy of Management Review*, *28*(2), 318–328.

13 McEachran, R. (2016). Funerals for failed startups that allow entrepreneurs to rise from the ashes. *The Guardian*. Retrieved from www.theguardian.com/small-business-network/2016/jul/29/funerals-failed-startups-entrepreneurs-rise-ashes

14 Weick, K. E., Sutcliffe, K. M., & Obstfeld, D. (2005). Organizing and the process of sensemaking. *Organization Science*, *16*(4), 409–421.

15 Morrison, J., & Meliza, L. (1999). *Foundations of the after action review process* (Special Report 42). Alexandria, VA: United States Army Research Institute for the Behavioral and Social Sciences.

9

CONVERSATIONAL APPROACHES FOR OTHER DILEMMAS OF FOUNDING TEAMS

Talking about sensitive topics

Making productive pivots is an important and predictable challenge that faces all innovative entrepreneurial teams. However, it is not the only such challenge; teams have an abundance of complicated and significant situations to navigate. Despite the difficulties that each challenge may pose, teams can rest assured that all challenges require thoughtful conversation – and having well-developed conversational competencies will help them manage whatever challenges emerge.

Noam Wasserman identifies several challenges that all early-stage entrepreneurial teams face in his book, *The Founder's Dilemmas: Anticipating and Avoiding the Pitfalls That Can Sink a Startup*.[1] He advocates that teams need to work through these predictably sticky issues deliberately rather than sleepwalk through them. However, there is a reason why teams try to sidestep them: They are sensitive subjects. Fortunately, the conversational moves that lead teams to success in other matters work for teams talking about these foundational topics too.

A central dilemma noted by Wasserman is the tension between wanting to generate maximum wealth versus wanting to maintain control of the venture. He is not alone in noticing this tension. One often-cited study of more than 1,000 entrepreneurs found that the top six motivating factors behind a founder's desire to start a venture were related to wealth or control.[2] Consequently, conversations related to equity allocation and team roles are among the most essential and the most difficult for teams to have with each other.

Co-founders should have a general conversation about each other's beliefs about wealth and control very early in the life of the venture. Understanding where you fall on that spectrum and where your partners fall can help you make decisions more peacefully in the future.

While there are many ways to open such a conversation one non-threatening one is to draw the following spectrum on a whiteboard (or another surface if no whiteboard is available):

$$\text{Rich} \longleftrightarrow \text{King/Queen}$$

With that image in sight, simply begin the conversation by asking each other where you fall between the two end points of Rich and King/Queen, as Wasserman[3,4] frames it. After each person has been able to affix a sticky note or other mark along the trajectory, the team can launch into dialogue.

By remembering that there are no right or wrong answers, and the point of the conversation is not to persuade anyone to change, you and your teammates will be able to learn something about each other. You might discover, for example, that everyone wants to be rich much more than they want to stay in control of the venture. If so, then you can anticipate that the co-founders will be agreeable to keeping a small slice of a large equity pie. On the other hand, you might discover that some founders see these motivating factors very differently. You might even find that some team members are not motivated by these particular factors at all and are driven by other concerns such as social responsibility. Having great differences between co-founders does not mean that the team is doomed to dysfunction, but it does mean that negotiations might take more time and require greater sensitivity.

The dilemmas that vex founding teams are many. Some of the most common ones include equity allocation, role definition and alteration, and founder departures. Team members also experience challenges outside of the workplace, such as a divorce or the death of a parent, while they are working on the venture. These personal matters can temporarily impact a person's ability or at least their availability to focus on work. The way that team members talk about all of these types of dilemmas can make a difference to the venture.

Equity allocation

Members of a founding team know that the ownership of the venture will be shared – with the other founders, with new hires yet to be named, and with investors. Talking about ownership of the venture is akin to talking about the value each team member is providing to the venture. Consequently, a conversation about equity allocation can make people uncomfortable. In an attempt to sidestep the unease about each founder's value to the venture, some founding teams might opt to split ownership equally. However, equal is probably not fair.

One way that a founding team comes to terms with this fact can be illustrated by the following story. Two co-founders, Jill and Chris, had worked together for years in a large technology company. Over time, the two of them developed an idea for an app. After she got some verbal encouragement from a venture capitalist whom she admired, Jill quit her job to explore the possibility of building a venture around this concept. Chris had two kids and could not quit until there was a source of income for him in the new venture. But he was willing to work on evenings and weekends for the time being.

Jill and Chris were both senior level people. Consequently, they both could contribute significant amounts of talent to the new venture. They saw each other as peers and real partners. This caused them to lean toward an initial 50/50 split of equity. However, Jill alone was taking the risk; she had quit her job and was willing to invest some of her savings – about $50,000 – to enable the pre-revenue phase of their venture. This presented them with a question: How could they treat Jill's contribution fairly in the equity split?

Chris thought that Jill could just loan the money and repay herself after the company could afford it. But Jill thought that approach failed to value the risk she alone was taking. Because she might never get the money back, she wanted it to be an equity transaction.

Awkward conversations about this topic became the focus of their meetings. Eventually, the two of them started to talk about hypothetical valuations of the venture. Their guiding logic was that their venture – their ideas and skills at this point – could be valued at $500,000. If Jill put in $50,000, then her investment would be valued at 10%. These calculations prompted Jill to suggest that she receive a bonus in the equity split; instead of 50/50 split, it would be 55 for her and 45 for Chris. At first Chris was reluctant to accept it; he thought that the venture would be nowhere without his contribution to the development of the product. But he finally came around when Jill reminded him that she was working full-time on the venture and was going without income until they either had paying customers or external funders.

Whether or not you would have struck the same deal that Jill and Chris did, it does sound like the two of them understood where they fell on the Rich-versus-King spectrum. They avoided haggling about equity because they were more interested in having a modest piece of a robust venture than having a big piece of something small.

Allocating equity amicably, as Jill and Chris were able to do, is aided by the use of interpretive language. Collaborative language forms – such as heedfulness and equal participation – demonstrate real respect for everyone involved. And that respect for each other is essential. Otherwise, people can feel like equity allocation is a statement of their worth as a person. Using collaborative language to navigate these ownership conversations can keep everyone feeling valued. Provisional language forms such as conditional verbs and improvisational skills can help people authentically explore various ways of cutting up the equity pie. And reflective language forms – such as the ability to suspend a conversation – can help teams manage emotions and stay curious about discovering optimal ways to structure the ownership for the team's future.

Usually, the conversations about equity come early in the life of a venture. Soon after come conversations about roles.

Defining and reassigning roles

It is a common source of founder concern: the partners from the venture capital firms will come on board and replace the founder CEO. But that is not the only time that roles and responsibilities need to be considered. Early on, innovative entrepreneurial teams need to decide on their own what each person does (not just each person's title). And over time, teams must proactively make changes to those job descriptions when skills, titles, and organizational needs no longer align.

Again, interpretive language can help teams establish a framework for talking about roles and to eventually make necessary changes to roles.

When initially carving out roles maintaining a provisional stance can be useful. Job descriptions are not fixed in stone, and specifying responsibilities in conditional language helps to make that point. Later on, conditional language can help team members whose jobs are changing redefine their roles in ways that are rewarding to them and the venture.

One of the reasons that role changes are so dreaded by team members is that changes are too often something that is done *to* someone rather than *with* someone. If everyone has been doing good work, but the efforts just need to be redirected to enable the venture to ascend then there is no reason to approach a conversation about a role change as if you were firing the other person (or being fired yourself). Instead, teams that authentically use collaborative language – first-person plural and heedfulness – can turn role change conversations into opportunities to co-create a new, mutually beneficial assignment for a team member.

The key here, however, is authenticity. As soon as a team member feels devalued or disrespected there is no magic word that will instantly restore a sense of shared well-being. If you find yourself angry at the other person or wanting to force him or her into a different role then you will want to find your own humility – some compassion – before engaging in that exchange.

Sometimes when the role no longer fits, a founder might choose to leave a young company. Managing team member exits is another situation that requires interpretive conversation.

A NOD TO RESPECTFUL INTERACTIONS

Respect for teammates and employees is a key part of the lean startup approach. One of the main ways we show respect at work is through our verbal interactions. The language of ongoing regard expresses appreciation and admiration through direct, specific, and non-attributive communication.[5] Direct communication of praise is a positive act that most of us probably can, and do, do without a second thought. Communicating your appreciation for a teammate's contribution directly to him or her instead of through someone else enhances the sincerity of the message for the recipient. Offering specific as opposed to generic praise might require a little more forethought. While it might be easier to give blanket praise (e.g., You did great), specific praise (e.g., Your knowledge of the technology really helped us close the deal) has greater and longer-lasting impact for the recipient. Giving non-attributive affirmation might be the most difficult aspect of practicing the language of ongoing regard for most people. Even though we mean well when we offer attributive praise (e.g., You are so smart), we are passing a kind of judgment about who and how the person is when we make such statements. Consequently, non-attributive affirmation that avoids assertions about the recipient's character or innate abilities tends to be more effective.

Helping the remaining team after someone leaves the venture

An innovative entrepreneurial team can undergo significant changes to its personnel structures, sometimes with little warning. Team members might want more certainty in their work life when they become parents. Or they might have to move to a different city when a spouse gets a dream job or one of their parents needs elder care.

When one team member is opting to leave while the team is making progress and feeling good, some of the conversations about the exiting process are not very complicated. Topics discussed tend to lean toward preparations for the next person in the role (e.g., document the work that he or she has done and possibly train the next person) and plans for a farewell party. A conversation about equity also must occur. These, too, can be without tension – if handled thoughtfully.

What to talk about with regard to equity when a team member opts to leave is covered in many books and websites about founder's agreements. *How* you talk about the matter is equally important. Much as in the case of equity allocation the ongoing team and the departing team member will both fare better if the conversation maintains a collaborative spirit. By striving to maintain an equal and heedful exchange everyone will be able to review the details about departures in the agreement in the most amicable way possible. And if the meaning of the agreed-on terms is understood differently in this circumstance by the parties involved, again, by maintaining an interpretive stance everyone will be better able to come to a shared understanding and peaceful resolution.

In fact, shared understanding is essential to optimal departures regardless of the originating factor driving the exit. Laying off or firing a team member is never pleasant for anyone involved on either side of the matter. The same can be said when a team member quits because of bad blood. In these circumstances, perhaps more than in any other, the language used in these departure conversations matters a lot.

As negotiation advisors will tell you, being clear and compassionate is vital when letting someone go.[6] So this is a meeting in which heedfulness, in particular, will serve you well.

The day when someone leaves the office for the final time is an occasion for a conversation with the remaining team. Simultaneously reflective and forward-looking, productive post-departure team meetings tend to benefit from the use of first-person plurals, levity, and humility. This is especially true when a team must process an untimely departure of a team member. For example, when Daniel Lewin, one of the core members of the Akamai team, died aboard one of the planes that hit the World Trade towers on 9/11, the remaining team had to grapple with the loss of their friend, the meaning of his absence for the future of the company, and the practicalities of honoring his stake in the venture. Needless to say, the conversations related to Lewin's absence were sensitive and required heedfulness writ large.

Whenever disruptions in team composition occur, it is helpful for a team to have already established a shared understanding of the roles and responsibilities of all team members. This collective mental representation of the organization is not an org chart. Instead, it is a dynamic understanding of who does what; it is a virtual role system.[7]

A clear example of a virtual role system in action is described in Weick's account of the Mann Gulch disaster, a forest fire that had dire consequences for the firefighting team. The fire-fighting team had at least three roles: leader, second-in-command, and crewmember. The leader went first in line, assessed the situation, gave orders, and selected routes, including escape routes. The second-in-command trailed the crew through the forest and repeated the leader's orders, confirmed the crew's comprehension of orders, and helped the crewmembers coordinate their work in real time. The crewmembers' role was to follow the orders and attempt to execute the tasks related to extinguishing – and surviving – the fire.

The language aspect of the team's work gave them a working role system. If, for example, the second-in-command should become incapacitated by the fire, one of the crewmembers could assume the role. Even without formal training in serving as the second-in-command, all crewmembers would have had an intuitive understanding of that role and how to do it in order to support the team.

The language patterns used in firefighting are far more routinized than those used by an innovative entrepreneurial team. However, even white-collar business meetings have language forms related to role systems. For example, one person might hold the official or unofficial responsibility of facilitator if he or she tends to start and stop meetings, keep the agenda, and garner participation among other things.[8,9] Or someone else might hold the official or unofficial responsibility of customer service representative if he or she tends to be the one who answers the phone or responds to customer concerns online.

It turns out that innovative entrepreneurial teams can use language to help develop their virtual role systems and become more resilient. For example, teams that strive for equal participation – in terms of turns taken, total words spoken, and questions asked in their team meetings – seem to build more robust collective models of teamwork. And having this richer model seems to help these teams achieve their shared goals regardless of changes to the team's structure. By maintaining a shared mental model of the roles and responsibilities through their patterns of communication, team members have a template to work from if key roles become vacant. In other words, conversational competencies help the remaining team members in their efforts to build a successful venture despite the changes in personnel.

The space between homelife and work life is thin

Founders of innovative entrepreneurial teams are first and foremost people. And just like the rest of the population, entrepreneurs occasionally experience disruptions in their personal lives. Some disruptions are happy, such as expecting and having a healthy baby. However, others, such as a divorce or the death of a parent, cause distress.

Because founders tend to be very invested in the venture, they may not have developed a hard boundary between the worlds of work and home.[10] Technology, of course, contributes to the blur between work life and homelife; rare are the founders who have not checked e-mail in the middle of the night on their phones. The overlap between these worlds can seem to support productivity in some periods of a venture's existence. However, when a core member of the team is troubled, the overlap means the venture may experience some disruption too.

Most, if not all, founders set out to create a good place for people to work. In other words, they want to create a company that enables the people who work there to live a good and happy life while they are doing great work. Organizations that achieve this tend to foster positive interpersonal interactions in the workplace.[11] Verbally expressing compassion, demonstrating care, and offering support, for example, can help people to feel their best and do their best at work.[12] Dignity, self-confidence, and self-esteem have all been associated with meaningful interactions with teammates.[13,14,15] Verbal acknowledgements of personal concern during times of trouble serve as an affirmation of each other's humanity. These expressions signal genuine care and stimulate a sense of loyalty throughout the team.

While spirals of positive affect form when teammates respond with authenticity and empathy to each other, founders cannot leave this entirely to chance. Fairness and expectations also matter in the creation of a productive workplace, and at some point, a team must turn its attention to policies. No small, early-stage team wants to spend a lot of time (or money for legal advice) to create an enduring parental leave policy or a bereavement policy because of one teammate's situation. However, if your team needs to invent a policy in response to a particular situation, then your collaborative, provisional, and reflective language skills can help you create a prototype of it. Provisional language, in particular, can help you articulate the temporary nature of the initial policy you are crafting.

Don't forget about the documentation process

The process of documentation is especially helpful in pivot-or-persevere meetings, but it also is useful in other challenging moments in the development of a young venture. For example, in equity allocation conversations, teams are grappling with a pressing question: How can we split the pie in a way that feels just to everyone on the founding team? You can use a question like that as the cornerstone of the documentation process. With your question articulated, you can start the notation process by putting relevant scaffolding on the whiteboard. The categories in an equity allocation conversation might include current ownership structure, contributions to date, contributions required in coming phase(s), current/proposed allocation, assumptions related to the allocation and the work, revised allocation, and current intended valuation for next round of funding.

After all the founders have had a chance to compose and affix their sticky notes, the team may opt to start the consolidation process by looking for ways to describe the contributions to date in similar terms (e.g., hours, dollars, etc.). This can lead into a conversation about contrasting sticky notes and the different impressions people have about the work. During the conversation, sticky notes should be revised or replaced to represent emerging ideas.

While discussing contributions and assumptions, it is important to use the conversational moves such as first-person plurals, levity, and heedfulness. You are exploring sensitive topics, and your goal is to understand and collaborate – not to persuade or dominate. The conversation should conclude with an articulation of a revised proposal on the matter of equity allocation for people to think about (not commit to on the spot). As you wrap up, take a moment to reflect on the exercise itself and to thank each other for thoughtfully engaging in the conversation. Then, take a digital photo of the artifact you have created and save it. When you reconvene to talk about the latest proposal for equity allocation, you may wish to start by looking at the artifact as a group.

While different scaffolding is required for every dilemma, founders who use the documentation process have a tool to help them address the main challenges that arise in the early days of a venture. The documentation process cannot tell you how to solve the problems that you face, but it does give you a reliable and constructive way to find workable solutions.

Interpretive language as an asset

The way your team talks can help you navigate any number of difficult situations. This chapter has revealed the ways that collaborative, provisional, and reflective language can help you productively grapple with some of the most common dilemmas that face innovative entrepreneurial teams. The next chapter connects interpretive language not with an isolated challenge but with the enduring nature of your venture's organizational culture.

Chapter takeaways

Founding team dilemma	How to talk about it	Tips
Equity allocation	Provisional language can facilitate conversations about hypothetical agreements.	Use the Rich-versus-King or Queen spectrum to understand your teammates' priorities. Use the documentation process to reveal assumptions about the value of contributions and to revise allocation balance.
Defining and/or reassigning roles	Language of ongoing regard can respectfully ease people through changes that cut close to their identity.	Direct, specific, and nonattributive compliments are most effective. Use the documentation process to reveal assumptions associated with roles and identity and to reframe positions and responsibilities.
Reenergizing the remaining team after departures	Heedful language	Use first-person plurals, levity, and humility; strive for equal participation. Use the documentation process to expose the concerns people may have and propose ways to address them.
Responding to the emergent homelife challenges of your team's members	Provisional language can help you craft early and temporary versions of guidelines for one that eventually will become policies for all.	Use the documentation process to recognize assumptions and articulate the reasons behind the contours of the temporary policy. Use language to convey compassion, care, and camaraderie.
Using the documentation process to navigate these and other dilemmas that face your team	Tap into your collaborative, provisional, and reflective language abilities while you make your interpretations visible.	Isolate the core question to drive your documentation process; then dive in.

Questions for my team

How often do we use collaborative, provisional, and reflective language when we are talking through a dilemma (e.g., allocating equity, defining roles, etc.)?

Are there dilemmas on the horizon that we could talk about in a new way – possibly by engaging in the documentation process?

What do we usually write on the whiteboard when we are talking through a dilemma? How could we use the documentation process in these situations?

Notes

1 Wasserman, N. (2012). *The founder's dilemmas: Anticipating and avoiding the pitfalls that can sink a startup*. Princeton, NJ: Princeton University Press.
2 Ibid.
3 Wasserman, N. (2006). Rich versus King: Strategic choice and the entrepreneur. [Best Paper]. *Academy of Management Proceedings*.
4 Wasserman, N. (2017). The throne vs. the kingdom: Founder control and value creation in startups. *Strategic Management Journal*, *38*(2), 255–277.
5 Kegan, R., & Lahey, L. (2001). *How the way we talk can change the way we work: Seven languages for transformation*. Jossey-Bass.
6 Stone, D., Bruce, P., & Heen, S. (1999). *Difficult conversations*. New York, NY: Viking/ Penguin.
7 Weick, K. E. (1993). The collapse of sensemaking in organizations: The Mann Gulch disaster. *Administrative Science Quarterly*, *38*(4), 628–652.
8 Barske, T. (2009). Same token different actions: A conversation analytic study of social roles, embodied actions, and ok in German business meetings. *Journal of Business Communication*, *46*(1), 120–149.
9 Rixon, A., McWaters, V., & Rixon, S. (2006). Exploring the language of facilitation. *Group Facilitation: A Research and Applications Journal*, 7, 21–30.
10 de Mol, E., Pollack, J., & Ho, V. (2018). *What makes entrepreneurs burn out*. Cambridge, MA: Harvard Business Publishing – Education, Harvard Business School Press.
11 Cameron, K. S., Dutton, J., & Quinn, R. E. (2003). *Positive organizational scholarship: Foundations of a new discipline*. Berrett-Koehler Publishers.
12 Powley, E. H., & Cameron, K. S. (2006). Organizational healing: Lived virtuousness amidst organizational crisis. *Journal of Management, Spirituality & Religion*, *3*(1–2), 13–33.
13 Dutton, J. (2003). *Energize your workplace: How to create and sustain high-quality connections at work* (Vol. 50). John Wiley & Sons.
14 Kahn, W. (1990). Psychological conditions of personal engagement and disengagement at work. *Academy of Management Journal*, *33*(4), 692–724.
15 O'Toole, J. (1973). *Work in America*. Cambridge, MA: MIT Press.

10

ORGANIZATIONAL CULTURE AND LANGUAGE

What organizational culture is

We've all heard the quip attributed to Peter Drucker about culture eating strategy for breakfast. Intuitively we probably all agree with that concept, but practically we may be at a loss about what to do with it. To build and maintain an organizational culture that supports innovative entrepreneurship you must first understand what culture is and the conditions that enable it. Once that foundation has been established you can think productively about team formation and development – and use interpretive language to shape an organization that will be poised to ascend.

Your team, like all founding teams, is a social system. It is probably small. Its membership may change and ideally grow. Its members may be hammering out early-stage ideas or helping out real customers. But an entrepreneurial team despite its size, stability, or stage of development is a dynamic organization made up of specific people. Moreover, that collection of people is recognized by members (and, at some point, nonmembers) as an entity.

To be clear, by *entity* I am not referring to legal status. Whether or not a team has formally filed to become an S Corp, LLC, or 501(c)(3), an entrepreneurial team is an entity because members know who is part of the team and who is not. Similarly, team members can have interactions in the world on behalf of the team.

This entity – the emerging venture – has a set of norms and practices that members follow. Early on these ways of acting and interacting rarely are expressed explicitly, but they are still present. These unspoken but shared ways of working are the beginnings of an organization's culture.

While many scholars and practitioners have offered an array of definitions of organizational culture, most definitions incorporate aspects of Edgar Schein's observation: Culture is expressed through materials, values, and assumptions.[1] Materials can be thought of as the physical objects that a team produces or uses to produce its shared work. They are associated with practices and privileges – such as all having access to particular files on a remote server – that enable the team to function as one. Values are shared beliefs about the team, the industry, and the world that enable teammates to feel connected to each other and to the goals of the team. And assumptions are tacit understandings about who you are as a team, including who knows what and who to go to for what.

Because organizational culture is so complex, it may be impossible to consciously design every aspect of it. But every entrepreneurial team – including yours – can influence the contours of its culture by investing in the conditions that enable optimal performance.

Conditions that foster productive teamwork

The basic idea behind creating conditions that enable desired outcomes can be illustrated by examples from personal wellness. If you as an individual wish to be healthy, you could approach your wellness in a variety of ways. In a reactive mode, you would seek help for pain or problems, taking therapies and other drugs (as prescribed) to treat issues as they arise. Alternatively, you could take a preventative approach. You could try to eat right, get exercise, and sleep well. Quite a few of us also might take a declarative stance. Unfortunately, saying that we intend to eat well, for example, without adhering to the behaviors associated with the preventative approach will not yield the results we seek.

Most people probably do a mix of reactive and preventative (and even declarative) care when dealing with their own health. But the prevailing wisdom says that the best path to wellness comes from preventative care – from creating the conditions that promote good health. Even though there is no guarantee of lifelong wellness – accidents, inherited traits, and other factors take their toll on everyone – taking good preventative care of our health makes a positive difference in the quality and length of our lives.

Something similar could be said for organizational wellness. Investing in the cultural conditions that enable optimal team performance tends to yield the best outcomes. Unfortunately, many entrepreneurs rely on reactive and declarative means to shape their team's organizational culture.

Six conditions are considered to be the most essential in the creation of a culture for high performance regardless of the nature of the organization.[2,3,4] These conditions, adapted for an entrepreneurial context, are the following:

1   The team needs clear boundaries that separate members from nonmembers, stability in that membership, and a shared task with interdependencies.
2   The team needs a meaningful purpose that engages the actions and attention of the members.

3   The teammates need to have the appropriate skills, talents, and dispositions to accomplish their shared goals.
4   The team needs to be part of a supportive ecosystem and have access to necessary resources.
5   The team needs access to competent and thoughtful coaching that responds to the team's specific needs over time.
6   The team must engage in norms of conduct that are appropriate for the team's specific profile, task, and environment.

The first three factors are the typical pieces of advice that are given to aspiring entrepreneurs as they form teams. Getting the who and the what as right as possible helps all teams ascend. Similarly finding ways to establish a sense of belonging – by naming the team, for example – helps people develop a commitment to each other and to the group.

The fourth factor speaks to the importance of an individual's personal support system as well as to the availability of professional resources such as venture capital. Founders need to be in a good place in their personal lives – socially, emotionally, physically, and financially – in order to withstand the challenges of a young venture. Moreover, they will need external support, and the closer they are to essential resources the easier it will be for the team to access them.

The fifth factor indicates the benefits that can come from participation in educational experiences as well from mentoring relationships. Recent research suggests that teams involved in accelerators rather than incubators even within an academic institution tend to have better outcomes.[5] This benefit might come from the expectation of hitting goals within a limited time frame paired with the appropriate guidance that are part of the accelerator experience. Incubators with their more casual approach do not impart the same benefit on teams. Similarly, teams are likely to benefit just as much if not more from building a developmental network as they are from participating in a traditional mentorship program.[6] By looking toward a variety of people as possible mentors, people seem to be able to get the assistance they need when they need it. Although formal mentor relationships are supposed to provide this support, not all mentor/mentee bonds are a very good fit – and even the ones that are basically a good fit cannot address every need that an aspiring entrepreneur will have. In other words, entrepreneurs seem to find high-quality coaching more easily through accelerators and developmental networks than they do through other means.

ON COACHING

We often associate entrepreneurship with advisors and mentors. Rarely do we think of coaches. What's the difference?

Advisors are seasoned allies who receive a stake in the venture in exchange for sharing their expertise and connections. They have an ongoing and evolving relationship with the founders and the venture. Advisors can provide direct benefits to a venture by opening doors to specific partnerships. Moreover, an advisory board made up of well-respected leaders can lend an air of credibility to a young startup.

Mentors might have a long-term relationship with a venture, but they do not tend to have a stake in the company. Consequently, they may be accessed on more of a transactional basis. Founders go to mentors for answers to specific questions, for example, how to model their financials better or how to close a sale. Mentors are called on to help founders solve discrete problems that stem from a simple lack of knowledge.

Coaches probably do not have a stake in the company either, but they do have an ongoing connection and a deep level of involvement with a team. Coaches provide individualized scaffolding to help founders learn from their experience as entrepreneurs. The orientation of coaching changes based on the evolving circumstances of the team. For example, at the beginning of a project, a good coach will provide responsible encouragement to the team. At the midpoint, a good coach will help a team process lessons learned so far and tweak their approach if necessary. And at the end of a project, a good coach will help the team with the task of making sense of the experience that they have just had, of harvesting knowledge to use again in the future.[7]

In other words, coaching is not about opening specific doors or lending credibility, nor is it about solving discrete problems that arise. It is an explicitly educational relationship that helps a team develop awareness and competencies over time anchored in their own experiences.

Cultivating a developmental network, including a set of coaches, is important to founders. Developmental relationships help an individual grow professionally and personally.[8] Connections with people from across a founder's personal and professional life provide opportunities for learning and for generating positive affect.[9,10]

And the sixth and final factor touches on the importance of establishing positive standards for intra-team interactions. Norms of conduct outline the behaviors that team members do and do not want in their meetings (or in their workplaces more generally). By establishing explicit norms teams can create experiences that are more efficient and enjoyable. Explicit norms also can help build a shared sense of accountability; if someone acts outside of a norm, another team member is more likely to speak up and get the team back on track if norms have been articulated in advance.

Interpretive language is a norm

Norms can be about many things. No cell phones in team meetings might be an articulated norm for some teams. Or text if you are going to be late might be an important norm for other teams to declare. It is important to note that team norms are not rules imposed on people. They are guidelines that often emerge out of team interactions and have buy-in from all team members.

Language forms also can be a norm. Some teams, for example, swear in team meetings, and others do not. No one put up a sign about a swearing policy; no one probably even mentioned it. However, the team has established a verbal way of being with regard to swearing. But that is not to say that norms about language have to be intuited.

If you wish to make interpretive language a norm, having a visible cheat sheet or a formal conversation about collaborative, provisional, and reflective language can be a very constructive thing for teams to do. By keeping a chart of the language norms visible it can help people remember to use them or to intervene if someone veers from them. Similarly, if you explicitly talk about the desire to use interpretive language in your meetings that conversation can remind people of the spirit of the team.

This is why checklists in professional settings became so popular a few years back. Whether their power is as a memory aid or as a social connection aid, checklists seem to help action teams do their work better.[11] Surgical teams, for example, use checklists to ensure that all necessary equipment is ready for the procedure. They also use them to make sure that everyone is focused on the procedure, knows everybody's name and responsibilities, and feels psychologically safe enough to speak up in the operating room if they sense that an error is about to happen. In other words, by talking about communication and the importance of speaking up despite differences in status, surgical teams become better teams.[12] Teams that talk about talking accomplish their surgical procedures with greater safety and with better patient outcomes.

While I am not advocating that entrepreneurial teams use a checklist at the start of every meeting, I do believe that talking about talking can have cascading benefits in entrepreneurial settings. And it is never too late – or too soon – to talk about talking with your team.

When culture starts

How a team gets started can influence what transpires over time. Some research indicates that key features of a team's cultural identity take shape within minutes of the team's first meeting.[13] In these earliest shared experiences, team members are defining who is on (and not on) the team, establishing roles, and formulating norms for the team's interactions.[14] Most of these activities happen in the background while the team is focused on other matters: Getting to know each other at a personal level and engaging in the work that has brought them together.

When teams are able to lay the groundwork for a healthy culture in their initial interactions, they position themselves for better outcomes. Those who get off to a good start immediately will face fewer internal issues over the life of the venture, and they will be more resilient when they do encounter internal or external challenges.[15]

This knowledge about team building and the creation of organizational culture is widely understood in the general business world. This is why many companies have special training sessions for new hires, offsite meetings for work groups at the start of new projects, and retreats for executives in advance of articulating new corporate strategies. However, within the world of entrepreneurship, other ideas tend to reign.

The typical advice given about forming an innovative entrepreneurial team is related to its composition. Founders are advised to find teammates they like: Teammates who are honest, emotionally grounded, and share the same vision.[16] Always, founders are encouraged to find teammates with complementary functional skills and past success in an entrepreneurial venture. This, in some cases, is the main advice given to student entrepreneurs participating in experiential learning activities such as university-sponsored entrepreneurship contests.

Universities and other organizations that host experiential learning activities for budding entrepreneurs often kick off a contest with a public event. The event includes presentations about the contest's rules, deadlines, and stories from past winners. The topics of team building and organizational culture sometimes are covered only superficially, mostly as part of the past winners' stories. Contestants are invited to use contest-related mixers and matchmaking websites to find co-founders.

Mixers are fun and provide a chance to meet people who are interested in doing entrepreneurship and in participating in the contest. They are promoted as social events and attract dozens if not hundreds of people. It is possible that you could meet someone who would complement you (and your partners if you have any at that point) at a mixer. However, it can be hit and miss. And even if you find someone who seems promising you might have focused only on determining if his or her area of expertise matches your team's current needs.

Matchmaking sites let founders search online for co-founders based on specific criteria. Some universities add a "Find Your Team" section to their Facebook pages or host their own matchmaking web pages. Others use online services such as CoFoundersLab (www.cofounderslab.com) or Founder2be (www.founder2be.com) to bring people with promising venture ideas together with talented individuals with an interest in joining a team. In most of these cases, the prompts that enable people to find each other and determine a fit tend to be based on area of expertise and geography.

Despite the focus on expertise, language and culture also are playing a role in mixers and matchmaking sites. From the initial introductory description of your venture – aloud at an event or in text form online – you are establishing the culture for your emerging organization. While it would be odd for you to talk in detail about verbal competencies at a mixer or to include that in your matchmaking post, you should be aware that you are at some level being assessed by others based on your verbal approach. Moreover, you might want to bring your own awareness of conversational competencies to the forefront as you consider candidates for your team (or as you consider teams to join).

What to look (or listen) for

While no one can be fully aware of a conversation's dynamics while a conversation is taking place, you can bring a sensitivity to certain conversational markers. For example, at a mixer if one person is telling you everything about the venture while her co-founder says nothing, that might be a red flag. There could be other explanations of course – the one person has a hearing issue or is very introverted, for example. But nevertheless, lopsided expressiveness is something to notice as it could indicate a cultural dynamic that would be inconsistent with resilience.

Verbal features to monitor on yourself whether you are looking to add team members include the following:

- Say *we*, and express appreciation especially for the existing team and for advisors and others in the ecosystem as well.
- Be curious about and interested in understanding the potential teammate's hopes, feelings, and interests in addition to asking them about their functional skill set.
- Acknowledge the information that potential teammate is sharing by building on what they have just said; ask clarifying questions or make connections between their statement and your approach.
- Use the language of ongoing regard by offering detailed, specific, and non-attributive affirmation to the potential teammates.

Other verbal features to be aware of when you are looking for a team to join include the following:

- Talking over each other or other imbalances of participation. If the current members of the team keep talking over each other (or over you) that might mean everyone is so in sync and enthusiastic that they finish each other's sentences. However, it also could indicate an organizational culture that lacks respect for everyone's contributions. Similarly, if one person talks more than the others, it might be because that is his or her area of expertise (e.g., the technologist talks more about the technology while the marketing person talks more about the market). However, it also could mean that one person is dominating the team's interactions and culture.
- Taking excessive credit. If a founder claims to be moving mountains by him- or herself, the person might be due a lot of credit and in need of a partner. However, it also might mean that the lead entrepreneur lacks a healthy sense of humility and underplays the contributions of others.
- Offering exceptional specificity. If a founder asserts that customers want very specific features or that sales will occur on very specific dates, for example, he or she may be very far along in the build–measure–learn cycle. However, he or she also might be imposing a false certainty on the situation and lack the agility that innovative entrepreneurship requires.

- Dwelling on credentials. If a founder is emphasizing the pedigrees of the existing team members or the accolades of the prototype, he or she may be trying to impress or persuade you. That might be okay, but it also might be another indication of an inability to integrate feedback and evolve the product and strategy.

Choosing to add a teammate or join an entrepreneurial team is an important decision. However, it is just the first step in the co-creation of a new venture. Teams must continually cultivate a productive culture for the company as it evolves.

Maintaining a positive organizational culture

Establishing and maintaining an organizational culture is an ongoing process for every team. A new venture's culture is constructed in every interaction and also contextually renewed over time. Meeting by meeting (and even turn by turn in each conversation) teammates are enacting the norms of their shared culture while also reinforcing (or evolving) it.

Scholars of positive organizational culture have found that teams who express and experience kindness, generosity, and humor at work tend to achieve higher levels of performance than those who do not.[17] Honest interactions in which teammates can be vulnerable enough to share authentic concerns also have been linked to good organizational outcomes.[18] And helpful and supportive interactions have been deemed essential to the social machinery of a well-functioning organization.[19]

All these aspects of a productive culture are communicated verbally. Collaborative language can help your team enact the psychological safety that allows teammates to voice authentic concerns. It also lends itself to the heedfulness that is experienced as kindness and generosity. Provisional language can help your team use humor productively. And reflective language forms can protect your team from overconfidence and enable you to value each other's opinions in ways that are internalized as helpful and supportive.

Collaborative, provisional, and reflective language also can help your team maintain its norms when they are breached, either knowingly or accidentally. These interpretive language forms give you the ability to clarify what a teammate has said and constructively address interactions that seem to betray the norms of the group. By heedfully inquiring about the intent or meaning of a perceived breach, you can repair misunderstandings or correct aberrations from the norm without creating more disruption.

Your conversations are the means by which team members affirm contributions that constitute your culture. They also are the means by which team members correct or reject comments and actions that are outside of the expected and acceptable norms. Through your conversations, your team establishes and evaluates what is possible to know, what is acceptable to know (and not know), and what levels of sustained uncertainty are permissible.[20,21]

Chapter takeaways

Cultural task	Elements of the task	Tips related to the task
Creating and maintaining your organizational culture	Conversation reflects your venture's culture while simultaneously creating its culture. Organizational culture includes norms of interaction.	Use collaborative, provisional, and reflective language to express kindness, humor, and generosity.
Cultivating a developmental network	Recognize people in your personal and professional circles from whom you can learn either formally or informally (as coaches, mentors, or advisors).	Ask for perspectives from people you've come to value and enjoy. Be ready to act as an informal coach to others in your network.
Looking for new teammates	Culture starts within minutes of people interacting.	Strive to verbally convey respect, appreciation, and inclusiveness through first-person plurals and equal participation.
Selecting a team to join	Consider how the existing teammates talk to and about each other; consider how they talk about their accomplishments and goals.	Listen for instances of collaborative, provisional, and reflective language as the team talks about its work and its goals; pay attention to who is talking (and why other team members may not be).

Questions for my team

How are we talking about the venture when we interact with potential new teammates?

What are some of the verbal norms we've developed for our team meetings? Are there any norms we'd like to change or add?

How does the culture of our venture feel different from the cultures of other teams you've been a part of? Do we like our culture, or are there some ways we could improve it?

Notes

1 Schein, E. H. (1992). *Organizational culture and leadership* (2nd ed.). San Francisco, CA: Jossey-Bass.
2 Hackman, J. R. (2002). *Leading teams: Setting the stage for great performances.* Boston, MA: Harvard Business School Press.

3 Hackman, J. R. (2012). From causes to conditions in group research. *Journal of Organizational Behavior, 33*(3), 428–444.

4 Wageman, R., & Gordon, F. M. (2005). As the twig is bent: How group values shape emergent task interdependence in groups. *Organizational Science, 16*(6), 687–700.

5 Aulet, W. (2014). Avoid stagnation: Acceleration Trumps incubation. Paper presented at the SXSW, Austin, TX.

6 Higgins, M. C., & Kram, K. (2001). Reconceptualizing mentoring at work: A developmental network perspective. *Academy of Management Review, 26*(2), 264–288.

7 Hackman, J. R., Wageman, R., Ruddy, T. M., & Ray, C. L. (2000). Team effectiveness in theory and in practice. In C. L. Cooper & E. A. Locke (Eds.), *Industrial and organizational psychology: Linking theory with practice*. Hoboken, NJ: Wiley-Blackwell, 109 –129.

8 Higgins, M. C. (2000). The more the merrier: Multiple developmental relationships and work satisfaction. *Journal of Management Development, 19*(4), 277–296.

9 Higgins, M. C., & Kram, K. (2001). Reconceptualizing mentoring at work: A developmental network perspective. *Academy of Management Review, 26*(2), 264–288.

10 Ragins, B., & Kram, K. (Eds.). (2007). *The handbook of mentoring at work: Theory, research, and practice*. Thousand Oaks, CA: Sage Publications.

11 Gawande, A. (2010). *The checklist manifesto*. New York, NY: Penguin Books.

12 Edmondson, A. C. (2003). Speaking up in the operating room: How team leaders promote learning in interdisciplinary action teams. *Journal of Management Studies, 40*(6), 1419–1452.

13 Wageman, R., Fisher, C., & Hackman, J. R. (2009). Leading teams when the time is right: Finding the best moments to act. *Organizational Dynamics, 38*(3), 192–203.

14 Ginnett, R. (1993). Crews as groups: Their formation and their leadership. In E. Weiner, B. G. Kanki, & R. L. Helmreich (Eds.), *Cockpit resource management* (pp. 71–98). Orlando, FL: Academic Press.

15 Hackman, J. R. (2012). From causes to conditions in group research. *Journal of Organizational Behavior, 33*(3), 428–444.

16 Fertik, M. (2011, February 8). How to pick a co-founder. *Entrepreneurship Blog*. Retrieved from https://hbr.org/2011/02/how-to-pick-a-co-founder

17 Ramlall, S. (2008). Enhancing employee performance through positive organizational behavior. *Journal of Applied Social Psychology, 38*(6), 1580–1600.

18 Ashkanasy, N., & Hartel, C. (2014). Positive and negative affective climate and culture: The good, the bad, and the ugly. In B. Schneider & K. Barbera (Eds.), *The Oxford handbook of organizational climate and culture* (pp. 136–152). Oxford: Oxford University Press.

19 Peyrat-Guillard, D., & Glinska-Newes, A. (2010). Positive organizational potential, organizational commitment and organizational citizenship behaviour: A French/Polish comparison. *Journal of Positive Management, 1*(1), 47–64.

20 Buttny, R. (1993). *Social accountability in communication*. London: Sage.

21 Shotter, J. (1984). *Social accountability and selfhood*. Oxford: Blackwell.

PART 5

Learning beyond the book

While writing this book, I have talked with numerous innovative entrepreneurial teams and other members of the entrepreneurial ecosystem. This section shares some of the common questions that people have asked about conversational competencies and the exercises outlined in this book. It also invites you to get involved with other innovators and entrepreneurs who are interested in the role of interpretive language in entrepreneurial success.

11

YES BUT . . . COMMON QUESTIONS

Frequently asked questions

1 I understand the negative potentiality of the misperceptions about entrepreneurship that you mention, that teams trying to look entrepreneurial can end up being anything but. However, isn't there some real value to being sincerely bold, passionate, and fast?

There is nothing wrong with being authentically bold, passionate, and fast. However, if those are the only tools in your toolbox you may find some circumstances to be more challenging than more agile teams do. So while you should not try to hide your natural boldness, passion, and speed you should not be consumed with trying to act in those ways all of the time.

The interpretive language forms articulated in this book are not meant to prevent teams from acting in ways that are bold, passionate, and fast. They are meant to give teams more skills so that they can express situated humility, for example, at times when they are truly unsure.

By developing conversational competencies teams can respond more appropriately to the dynamic and uncertain circumstances that define the context of their work. Over time, these more appropriate responses can result in better pivots and greater success.

2 Don't I really just need more information? Or better teammates?

You might need more, different, or better information, but only if you are facing a technical challenge – a challenge that is resolved by knowing *more*.[1] The same can be said for different teammates; you might need more functional diversity if you lack critical know-how (e.g., you need to add an engineer if your team is all business people trying to invent a piece of technology).

If you are facing an adaptive challenge, however, you will need to know *differently*. You need to separate your assumptions from your actualities. This kind of transformational learning is hard; it is threatening to your identity, your team, and your shared project or venture. A well-designed holding environment makes it much easier. Transformative learning is at the heart of the lean startup philosophy and also the design thinking movement.

On the teammate matter, your team might need different or additional skills on board in order to ascend. But if you have the functional bases covered perhaps your team just needs to get better at working together. **The difference between a team of experts and an expert team is based in conversational competencies.**

3   I'm an individual inventor how do these conversational competencies apply my innovative entrepreneurial team of one?

Most successful innovative new ventures are founded by teams. So it might be a good idea to find some collaborators. But if you can't or don't want to explore that possibility right now, there are still ways that your work can be enhanced by developing your individual conversational competencies.

Even without co-founders, you may be in workplace situations that include some backstage interactions. For example, if you are working a shared office space, you are part of a kind of extended inter-organizational team. As you enact your work in that context, you will need to cooperate in some way with the people around you. Your language skills will help you do that. And as your venture ascends, you almost certainly will need to bring on additional people. Understanding how you talk about yourself and your venture will help you attract (and eventually retain) the people you want on your team.

Ed Schein once said that dialogue is central to all action.[2] Much as an architect has a dialogue with a building site, the clients, and with his or her own sensibilities and expertise,[3] an entrepreneur can have a dialogue with prospective customers and partners. Moreover, through reflection you can have an ongoing dialogue with your own abilities and vision while enacting your work. These conversational competencies can help you tease apart the habitual ways that you may your work – and help you discover new, more advantageous ways that enable agility and resilience.

4   Our team has been struggling for a while, and we just don't seem to see eye to eye. Is there any way to talk through that? Or should we just give up on this one?

The world of negotiation has many conversational tips for teams navigating discord: appreciative inquiry, thoughtful paraphrasing, and acknowledged affect.[4] Each of these approaches to teamwork relies on heedfulness, on expressing sincere concern and respect for teammates and their views. Heedful interactions, as noted in earlier chapters, are aligned with collaborative conversations. So by attending to the conversational moves that facilitate collaboration, such as the first-person plural and equal participation between speakers, you may be able to have more productive, or at least less-stressful, team meetings.

You also may want to remember to make use of the provisional language forms. Conditional framing can make room for an array of possible meanings and possible next steps. Consequently, provisional language forms can allow your teammates to clarify their understanding of different perspectives and potentially divergent goals. They also can help you imagine entirely new paths forward while staying grounded in the realities of your context.

If the intra-team discord has you thinking about ending the venture, it is important to talk about the possibility of shutting down the venture sooner rather than later. The verbal moves that enable teams to grow successfully also can be used to amicably shut a company down. Similarly, playing the *Toasted Marshmallow* game can help teammates make sense of a venture that did not work.

5   We've done everything you said – twice – and we still seem to be failing. What's with that?

As much as we all wish for a simple solution to challenges, the fact remains that innovative entrepreneurship is hard. It is unpredictable and, despite best efforts, always somewhat untamable. The language forms in this book give you an expanded repertoire of actions in the face of uncertainty. If your team uses these conversational moves and documentation exercises in your meetings, you will probably be more likely to succeed than if you do not use them. However, conversational competencies are another tool in your toolbox; they are not a magic bullet.

While the conversational competencies described in this book represent the latest thinking about the factors that enable an innovative entrepreneurial team to ascend, they are not fixed concepts. The theory of conversational competencies continues to be refined, and the techniques that provide the greatest aid to teams do too. Updates to the ideas and exercises will be made available at this book's companion website – www.innovatorsdiscussion.com.

In the meantime, I encourage you to play the *Toasted Marshmallow* game. (See the Appendix for the instructions and game cards.) Failing forward is something most successful entrepreneurs have had to learn how to do. By playing the game you and your teammates can gain some new insights that can carry you forward.

6   My team does a lot of work through email, over the phone, and occasionally on skype. Do these conversational competencies transfer communication beyond face-to-face meetings?

The short answer is that I have not done extensive research on that – yet – so I cannot be as confident about the conversational moves that are used by high- and low-performance teams in settings other than in-person meetings. That said, heedfulness and an attitude of healthy self-doubt (i.e., giving the other person the benefit of the doubt) are features of conversation that are associated with high-performance teams. These same features are echoed in the conventional wisdom about positive email exchanges and video conferences.

Because mediated conversations have less richness than direct, face-to-face conversations, they require very clear communication. This can be accomplished, in part, by how you talk. However, it also is accomplished by what you choose to talk about – or more specifically what you choose to not talk about. Consequently, complex topics such as unpacking assumptions may be better suited for in-person conversations.

7   Can I use these exercises with a project team inside of an established company?

Absolutely! Increasingly companies are encouraging their employees to be more entrepreneurial. However, all too often, the employees are just supposed to intuit what that means. The exercises and documentation process can help your team develop the interpretive skills and conversational competencies associated with innovative entrepreneurial work. A good starting point may be a simple recommendation; tell your team members to read this book. Then you can start to incorporate the exercises and documentation process into your ongoing meetings.

In the beginning, you may wish to devote a meeting with your team to the exploration of a single exercise. For example, your team can enact a particular exercise then share and discuss insights from the exercise. Similarly, you can lead the group through the documentation process then review their experience of making interpretation visible. Part of the message you will want to deliver is that these conversational competencies and structured activities can help teams productively manage challenging situations.

Sometimes, of course, teams dissolve. Projects end and people are reassigned to new ones. If your team reaches such a point, you may wish to play the *Toasted Marshmallow* game as a way to wrap up on a positive note.

8   I am a technology licensing officer at a university. How can I get academics and industry stakeholders to develop their capacity for interpretive conversations?

The technology licensing office at a university has an important, but difficult, role to play in the innovative entrepreneurial process. Often functioning in the role of matchmaker, the technology licensing office tries to find industry leaders with problems that can be solved by an invention developed by academics. Some universities host discovery sessions on a regular basis to showcase a particular invention to business-minded folks. By articulating the desired norms for interaction at the start of these sessions you can raise people's awareness of the power of language and encourage them to use more collaborative, provisional, and reflective language in their interactions. You also can point them to the website associated with this book where they can find information and exercises to help them develop their conversational competencies.

To the extent that you have faculty members participating in an accelerator, you can introduce them to this book's activities as part of the curriculum. The exercises and the documentation process are designed to coordinate with a practice-based approach to teaching entrepreneurship. Similarly, if your office is affiliated with fellows or entrepreneurs in residence, you can host a workshop for these individuals to introduce them to the importance of interpretive language forms in the success of early-stage innovative entrepreneurial ventures.

9　I'd like to try the documentation process with my team to make our pivot-or-persevere meeting visible. They have not read this book. So can you help me explain what documentation is and why they should give it a go?

The sidebars within the chapter on documentation should be enough to get team members engaged. However, five key points might be helpful to them:

1　A specific question guides the documentation process. In many cases, entrepreneurial teams will be inspired by the guiding question, "Should we pivot or persevere?" or "In what way should we pivot?" In other instances, teams might be using the documentation process to navigate other challenges of founding teams. Questions such as "How can allocate equity in a way that makes everyone feel recognized?" or "How can we reassign roles to address our current needs and limitations?" might orient the process on those occasions.

2　Documentation is a team activity. It requires all team members to collectively explore and analyze his or her own and the group's impressions and observations. Having multiple perspectives is essential to the process and the outcomes of the exercise.

3　The documentation process engages different ways of representing and expressing ideas and actions, including written words, visual displays, and conversational interaction.

4　Documentation is useful in the present. As the team's way of working becomes visible, it becomes an object the team can discuss. This ability to look at the work process while doing the work can help a team determine whether a pivot is necessary and, if so, which one.

5　Documentation is useful for the future. Each documentation process results in an artifact (the photo). These artifacts are a record of the team's work over time, and they can help the team make discoveries about their habitual practices. Ultimately, they can help a team improve the way they do their work.

10 How do we make use of these conversational competencies in our conversations with our extended team – with our advisors and investors, for example?

Using collaborative, provisional, and reflective language forms in your meetings with members of your extended team should serve you well. These conversational moves all are grounded in authenticity and are oriented toward positive organizational functioning. It is hard to imagine a meeting that would not be enhanced by thoughtful and attentive interaction.

While you might tell your extended team about the interpretive approach to your work that you are cultivating through language, you might not need to. Simply by using interpretive language you will model the verbal norms of your team and will influence your meetings with advisors and investors.

One caution: The interpretive language forms highlighted in this book are intended to support the backstage conversations between members of the same team in private. They are not intended to support front-stage interactions – public exchanges between members of different stakeholder groups. So while collaborative, provisional, and reflective language will help your team prepare a pitch for a potential investor, they are unlikely to serve you extremely well in the delivery of the pitch. (Pitching is a kind of performance and requires attention to some different rules of communication.)

11 I facilitate an accelerator at a university. How can I use this book and its exercises to help the students who have been accepted into our program?

Most accelerators have an informal curriculum to help each cohort of aspiring entrepreneurs to develop core abilities and build early-stage ventures. Many have been using a practice-based approach to encourage entrepreneurial learning. The collaborative, provisional, and reflective language forms support the core practices associated with entrepreneurial education (e.g., play, empathy, creativity, experimentation, and reflection).[5]

You certainly can introduce your students to this book and its exercises (and website) as part of their shared learning experience. Moreover, you can help them recognize the interpretive orientation of entrepreneurial work by giving them opportunities and time to engage in collaborative, provisional, and reflective (CPR) conversation in your group meetings. As the facilitator, you also can create cues in the environment that help to establish and maintain an interpretive culture with the accelerator.

Because every accelerator has its own informal curriculum, there is no single way to use this book with a cohort of aspiring entrepreneurs. One possible approach would be to assign the chapters in Part 2 as readings that are discussed in sessions with individual teams and the entire cohort. Then, you can guide the teams (individually or as part of a cohort experience) through the individual routines. Use the session(s) to build each team's awareness of its habitual ways of interacting – and encourage them to embrace more interpretive language forms.

You also may opt to assign the chapters in Part 3. With everyone aware of the ideas associated with interpretive language and the documentation process, you can lead the teams in a demonstration of documentation. To do this, you probably will need to attend a pivot-or-persevere meeting with each team. You will bring the sticky notes, camera, and other materials, and you will set up the whiteboard with the appropriate categories (current prototype, assets, new information, proposed pivot(s), assumptions, revised proposal(s), product and market intention, and intended outcome). Then guide the team in the use of the notation method and help them examine their assumptions. Use the session(s) to show teams how they can make their innovation process visible on their own – and how this process can help them make better pivots and become more competent entrepreneurs.

And, of course, you can host a game day. Invite teams in your university's entrepreneurial ecosystem (or your town's entrepreneurial community) to play the *Toasted Marshmallow* game. Afterward, you can lead a discussion about the lessons people draw from their entrepreneurial experiences. Depending on the participants, you can highlight aspects of failing forward after the closure of a venture, finding your way after the sale of a venture, or other relevant matters in the life of an entrepreneur.

In your role, you are able to help aspiring entrepreneurs make space in their work to actively cultivate interpretive skills. Often, aspiring entrepreneurs are celebrated for being clever in a pitch or for developing a new product feature quickly. And while these are not bad things to be able to do, individuals who wish to build careers as successful entrepreneurial leaders need to be able to demonstrate and foster interpretive interactions within their teams. The explanations, examples, and exercises in this book can give the learners in your accelerator some specific ways to build backstage conversational competencies.

12   I'm the lead entrepreneur of a three-person team. Are we too small in number to do these exercises in a formal way? And are there any pitfalls to these exercises or tips you can suggest so that my team can make the most of our documentation efforts?

Even two-person teams can do these exercises. In, fact, it is great to get into the habit of doing these routines when your team is small. You are creating a culture that makes time for thoughtful interpretation. When you add more people to your team, you will be able to use this way of being to make it easier for new folks to engage in your shared work.

There are some tips that could be helpful to remember. First, it is important to have enough time to do these exercises. If you have only 5 minutes to engage, you may not get very nuanced contributions. Similarly, it is important to take time to make sure you are understanding each other's perspectives and encouraging alternative views. Another tip: Do not let the exercises become a form of busy work. These activities are not to the side of your main work; they facilitate your main work. If you sense that people are offering superficial responses then it is worth reminding people of the goal of the exercises and identifying the reasons behind the shallow engagement. And last, do not forget to capture and keep the visible work you do. Having a portfolio of your documentation over time will help you lead your current venture through the pivots yet to come – and it will help you prepare for your future endeavors throughout the entrepreneurial ecosystem.

But perhaps the most basic thing to keep in mind is simply CPR. Collaborative, provisional, and reflective language can help you and your team navigate all of the challenges that founding teams face.

Notes

1 Heifetz, R. (1994). *Leadership without easy answers*. Cambridge, MA: Harvard University Press.
2 Schein, E. H. (2003). On dialogue, culture, and organizational learning. *Reflections*, 4(4), 27–38.
3 Schön, D. A. (1988). Designing: Rules, types and words. *Design Studies*, 9(3), 181–190.
4 Stone, D., Bruce, P., & Heen, S. (1999). *Difficult conversations*. New York, NY: Viking/Penguin.
5 Neck, H. M., Greene, P. G., & Brush, C. (2014). *Teaching entrepreneurship: A practice-based approach*. Northampton, MA: Edward Elgar Publishing.

12

A COMMUNITY TO HARNESS THE POWER OF WORDS

A kind of magic

This book began with a quote from the film, *Harry Potter and the Deathly Hallows (Part 2)*, one of J.K. Rowling's beloved stories. Wise and trusted Dumbledore offered protagonist Harry some advice: Words can be an "inexhaustible source of magic" (Copyright © Warner Brothers, 2011).[1,2]

Words can seem to work magic, indeed. They are the main way that people make sense of circumstances – including the shared circumstances of innovative entrepreneurial teams. How you talk about what is happening to and within your team will shape, in part, what can happen next. Your conversations hold the key to establishing, maintaining, and evolving what you do, how you do it, and who you become. They are an essential part of transforming your ideas into reality.

Words are powerful, and harnessing that power requires some training and support. Reading this book has gotten you started. This book has shared a set of exercises to help you develop collaborative, provisional, and reflective language (or CPR language, for short). It also has explained a documentation process that can help you make your team's interpretations visible now – and help you improve your entrepreneurial practice into the future. The book has pointed out how these conversational moves and the documentation process can help you navigate the main challenges that teams tend to face.

This book also serves as a gateway to a community of practice, a network of other people interested in developing their own conversational competencies.

Community of practice

While there is no mystical academy devoted to the development of entrepreneurs' verbal powers, there is a community of practice connected to the exploration of interpretive language and lean startup performance. You have already become a member of the community by taking an interest in the content of this book. New ways to participate are always taking shape, and one way to stay informed about opportunities and develop your skills can be found on the site affiliated with this book: www.innovatorsdiscussion.com.

The site keeps an updated list of events related to interpretive language and innovative entrepreneurial teamwork. It also includes additional exercises, materials, and tips to help you and your team develop your conversational competencies.

But as robust as the site may become, it presents only a sliver of the activities focused on interpretive language within entrepreneurial work that take place around the world. Accelerators, hackathons, meetup.com events, and other startup gatherings are available in nearly every university and every town these days. As more people are becoming aware of the role of language in innovative entrepreneurial work, more of these gathering places are devoting some attention to the verbal dynamics of teams. And if you have not come across a community of practice in your local area, then feel free to use your entrepreneurial verve to start one.

Additional resources

While I do hope you become an advocate for the role of language in innovative entrepreneurial work, I also would like to point you to related networks that share an interest in high-quality conversation. None of the following groups have a recommended set of conversational competencies for innovative entrepreneurs, but they do offer an approach to team processes that complement the main ideas of this book.

If you are primarily interested in social change ventures then you might enjoy learning about the following groups:

- Center for Civic Reflection (civicreflection.org)
- Interaction Institute for Social Change (interactioninstitute.org)
- MIT Co-Lab (colab.mit.edu)
- Presencing Institute (www.presencing.com)

If you have an interest in conversation as it relates to formal negation, then you might want to explore the materials and programs at the Harvard Law School Program on Negotiation (PON; www.pon.harvard.edu).

If the concept of organizational learning in general is appealing to you, then the Society for Organizational Learning (SOL; www.solonline.org) and some of the initiatives within Project Zero (www.pz.harvard.edu) may be relevant to your work.

People interested in team-based design thinking and prototyping may want to check out the resources available through the Stanford University Design School (dschool.stanford.edu). Its programs and videos can help teams of aspiring entrepreneurs improve their innovation skills. IDEO U also provides tips and a list of useful links on its site (www.ideou.com).

And the Center for Positive Organizations at the University of Michigan has a number of books and tools – including a game to help with brainstorming (positiveorgs.bus.umich.edu). These resources may be helpful to people interested in developing their general skills as a leader of a healthy organization.

People interested in learning more about appreciative inquiry will find books, resources, and other information at the AI Commons (appreciativeinquiry.champlain.edu).

Relevant written works

More information on the importance of externalizing insights in visible forms can be found at the Making Learning Visible section of the Harvard University Graduate School of Education's Project Zero website and in several written works on the subject: *Making Teaching Visible: Documenting Individual and Group Learning as Professional Development* (Project Zero, 2003); *Making Thinking Visible: How to Promote Engagement, Understanding, and Independence for All Learners* (Ritchhart, Church, & Morrison, 2011); and *Visible Learners: Promoting Reggio-Inspired Approaches in All Schools* (Krechevsky, Mardell, Rivard, & Wilson, 2013).

Other books that I have found helpful and may interest founders, educators, and scholars who are curious about language in action include the following:

- *Difficult Conversations*, by Doug Stone, Bruce Patton, and Sheila Heen
- *Teaming: How Organizations Learn, Innovate, and Compete in the Knowledge Economy*, by Amy Edmondson
- *How the Way We Talk Can Change the Way We Work: Seven Languages for Transformation*, by Robert Kegan and Lisa Laskow
- *How to Be a Positive Leader: Small Actions, Big Impact*, by Gretchen Spreitzer and Jane Dutton
- *Humble Leadership: The Power of Relationships, Openness, and Trust*, by Edgar Schein and Peter Schein
- *Innovation: The Missing Dimension*, by Richard Lester and Michael Piore
- *King Arthur's Roundtable: How Collaborative Conversations Create Smart Organizations*, by David Perkins
- *Opening the Door to Coaching Conversations*, by Linda Gross Cheliotes and Marceta Flemming Reilly
- *Teaming to Innovate*, by Amy Edmondson
- *Team Talk: The Power of Language in Team Dynamics*, by Anne Donnellon
- *Thanks for the Feedback: The Science and Art of Receiving Feedback Well*, by Doug Stone and Sheila Heen
- *The Five Languages of Appreciation in the Workplace: Empowering Organizations by Encouraging People*, by Gary Chapman and Paul White

- *The Founder's Dilemmas: Anticipating and Avoiding the Pitfalls That Can Sink a Startup*, by Noam Wasserman
- *Reclaiming Conversation: The Power of Talk in a Digital Age*, by Sherry Turkle
- *The Reflective Practitioner: How Professionals Think in Action*, by Donald Schon
- *The Secret Life of Pronouns: What Our Words Say About Us*, by James Pennebaker
- *Yes, And: How Improvisation Reverses 'No, But' Thinking and Improves Creativity and Collaboration*, by Kelly Leonard and Tom Yorton

While none of these books specifically features entrepreneurial teams or conversational details related to innovative entrepreneurial work, they all touch on themes that have repeatedly emerged in the previous chapters. They all, for example, recognize that productive workplace conversations are not about charismatic language, speedy decisions, or bold actions. They are marked instead by playfulness, heedfulness, and other conversational features essential to productive teamwork.

As you continue to develop your conversational competencies remember that interpretive language facilitates team success by making you more resilient. The more you incorporate CPR language into your entrepreneurial teamwork the more you will be able to transform unwanted interruptions to your plans into productive developments for your future.

No matter how your team talks, starting a new venture is full of challenges. But by using interpretive language – collaborative, provisional, and reflective conversational moves – your team can improve its ability to exchange information, ascribe meaning, and take action. Your team can position itself to ascend despite the dynamism and complexity of innovative entrepreneurial work. Interpretive language can help you reach your goals by unleashing your ability to recognize alternative possibilities, to make progress while avoiding premature commitments.

Entrepreneurship is a conversational accomplishment

In the early stages of a new venture – from the proverbial drawing on the back of a napkin until an initial product is ready for delivery – much, if not most, of what founding teams do is talk. Conversations about their shared tasks (What do our prospective customers want, and what resources can we harness to deliver that?), their condition (How are we doing as individuals and as a team?), and their possibilities (What are the best next steps for us to take?) allow innovative entrepreneurial teams to develop products, companies, and whole industries. **New products, new ventures, and all innovations are literally *talked into being*.**[3] Language is central to the ways that all people – including entrepreneurs – accomplish real work together in the real world.[4] Conversation is the primary link between individual participation in your team's work and the collaborative accomplishment of your new product or venture. Consequently, how your team talks can influence your venture's ability to ascend. Or, in other words, you can think of innovative entrepreneurial work as a conversational accomplishment.

As you know, innovative entrepreneurial work is a multifaceted practice that is steeped in uncertainty and reliant on interactions between people. Because of these dynamics, teams need to be skilled at using interpretive language. This book has described some of the "interactional machinery" behind successful teamwork.[5]

The verbal advantages that separate the best innovative entrepreneurial teams from the rest have been presented, chapter by chapter, in this book. The first section of the book introduced you to some of the limitations of the conventional wisdom about innovative entrepreneurial work. The book then described the conversational competencies that every innovative entrepreneurial team should master and offered tips on ways you can incorporate these language moves into your routine work.

Several routines were presented to help your team develop its interpretive skills through conversation:

- Tell Me More – encourages different perspectives
- Reconsidering Beliefs – stimulates additional inquiry
- Potentially Next – boosts the use of provisional framing
- Superhero Says – inspires levity and alternative framing
- Private Pivots – supports individual and group reflection
- We Are Here – guides reflection on potential pivots and activates provisional ways of knowing

Enacting these routines in your team meetings encourages the development of new insights about customer feedback. Consequently, these routines can help your team avoid premature cognitive commitments, build intra-team cohesion, and confidently take the next steps as you work to create new products and a new venture.

A central recommendation of the book is the documentation process. By developing a practice of documentation your team can learn to productively manage the many inflection points that confront entrepreneurs. Teams that make their interpretation visible through documentation are likely to benefit from it in real time. Pivots can be considered in all of their complexity, and changes to the prototype or the strategy can be undertaken with a confidence that is grounded in the details of the team's discussion. Moreover, by documenting their pivoting process, teams encourage participation, big-picture thinking, and group memory – dynamics that can help your team over time.

Teams also can benefit from playing the *Toasted Marshmallow* game. As players respond to the question cards and to their teammates' answers, they begin to process feelings, contextualize experiences, and reconsider professional identities and possibilities. You will hear your teammates' perspectives on the venture and think carefully about your own. Whether the *Toasted Marshmallow* game is played at the end of a venture or at another pivotal point, most participants find the game-based conversation to be surprisingly satisfying and energizing.

Cast your spell

As you build your awareness of collaborative, provisional, and reflective language, your conversational competency will improve. Your understanding of what entrepreneurship is and how entrepreneurship is done also may evolve. You may find that the process of documenting your team's innovation process allows you to know not only *what* the lean startup process is but also *how* to verbally enact it. Your insights – about your product, your venture, and your team – will position you to become a better entrepreneur. Each time you constructively communicate your new perspectives back into your workplace conversations, you will be actively contributing to the interpretive success of your team.

While this is not a book of incantations, it does provide you with everything you need to verbally talk your venture into being. Collaborative, provisional, and reflective language, the routines, the documentation process, and the *Toasted Marshmallow* game will help you transform your ideas into new products and new ventures. Your conversations are a never-ending source of promising possibilities for your current company and your entire entrepreneurial career. Your words, in essence, can work magic for your team today and across the entrepreneurial ecosystem over time.

Notes

1 Rowling, J. K. (2007). *Harry Potter and the deathly hallows*. New York, NY: Scholastic Press.
2 Yates, D. (Writer). (2011). Harry Potter and the deathly hallows, Part 2. In D. Heyman, D. Barron, & J. K. Rowling (Producer). USA : Warner Bros. Entertainment.
3 Heritage, J. (1984). *Garfinkel and ethnomethodology*. Cambridge: Polity Press.
4 Schegloff, E. A., Jefferson, G., & Sacks, H. (1977). The preference for self-correction in the organisation of repair in conversation. *Language, 53*, 361–382.
5 Sacks, H. (1984). Notes on methodology. In J. M. Atkinsen & J. Heritage (Eds.), *Structures of social action: Studies in conversation analysis*. Cambridge: Cambridge University Press.

AFTERWORD ON THE METHOD

Using unedited video and audio recordings of innovative entrepreneurial teams at work, the studies associated with this book use Conversation Analysis (CA) as their main methodological approach. CA is a micro-level examination of naturally occurring talk. Emerging from sociology and, more specifically, ethnomethodology, CA enables researches to uncover structures and patterns in conversation. It examines the meaning of the words as they are understood in real time by the speakers themselves. It considers the structure of each utterance and the work it does in that moment to advance a team's ability to accomplish its shared goals. In other words, Conversation Analysis examines *how* communication occurs; it considers the situated means by which team members accomplish their shared work.[1]

The principles of CA include the following:

- Talk is a primary means for accomplishing social action.
- Talk emerges in a specific context, and talk simultaneously creates that context.
- Talk and interaction have an order and logic.
- Talk and the order of turns can reveal how participants interpret the immediate context.
- Only recordings of naturally occurring conversation can provide authentic data suitable for inquiries into the observable details of interaction.

CA-oriented studies conducted within professional settings (often referred to as workplace interaction studies) have an additional requirement. Only analysts who have an authentic experience in the workplace context can adequately interpret the interplay between speakers, texts, and contexts.

This book also makes use of quantitative CA. After the data is analyzed qualitatively, the work each utterance is doing is compared with language forms in the literature (e.g., of sensemaking, teamwork, and other relevant domains of scholarly research). This is an iterative process of description, analysis, and interpretation. It involves listening to the recordings many times and updating the codebook accordingly. Eventually, a final codebook emerges. At that time, each utterance is associated with the final set of language forms, and the frequency with which each form appears is tallied. These tallies – these descriptive statistics – can enable comparisons between teammates and across teams.

To do this kind of analysis, researchers must have access to recordings of naturally occurring conversations in order to transcribe them and study them in exacting detail. The recordings associated with this book captured the naturally occurring conversations of early-stage innovative entrepreneurial teams enacting a lean startup approach to new venture creation. Names of all individuals, products, and ventures were changed to conceal their identities.

The studied teams ranged in size from two to five members. All of them were in very early stages; most of them had only first discussed their venture concepts with each other a few months before the data capture began. None of them had incorporated or had a fully functioning prototype or customer base before participating in the study. Few of them had had any prior exposure to an entrepreneurial workplace. All of them spoke fluent English, met in-person for most of their team meetings, received coaching in lean startup methods, had access to advisory networks, and were intent on building high-tech, high-growth ventures.

Scholars widely agree that no single formula for successful new venture creation will be discovered.[2,3,4] However, research is needed that can both "recognize variation in the phenomenon of organization creation, while also offering insights into how these diverse activities might lead to patterns of successful formation of organizations".[5] Such research falls with the scholarly domain of entrepreneurship-as-practice.

A practice approach shifts the focus from the entrepreneurs themselves to their shared activities and interactions.[6] It attends to the situated details of entrepreneurial work not simply to describe them, but to analyze the social machinery that enables teams to accomplish their immediate goals and (re-)create the ongoing contexts of entrepreneurship.[7]

CA-oriented studies, such as the ones in this book, contribute to our understanding of entrepreneurship as practice. They move the focus away from the general social skills of entrepreneurs[8,9] to the interactional and emergent nature of entrepreneurial identities, products, ventures, and communities[10,11,12] They also help to bridge the gap that exists between the theoretical work of scholars and the practical work of entrepreneurs.

If you would like to know more about the methodologies and how they contribute to the understanding of innovative entrepreneurial work, you may wish to consult *Practice Theory in Action: Empirical Studies of Interaction in Innovation and Entrepreneurship.*[13]

Notes

1 Psathas, G. (1995). *Conversation analysis: The study of talk in interaction*. Thousand Oaks, CA: Sage.

2 Gartner, W. B. (1985). A conceptual framework for describing the phenomenon of new venture creation. *The Academy of Management Review, 10*(4), 696–706.

3 Reynolds, P. (2007). New firm creation in the United States: A PSED 1 overview. *Foundations and Trends in Entrepreneurship, 3*(1), 1–150.

4 Weick, K. E. (1979). *The social psychology of organizing*. Random House.

5 Gartner, W. B., Carter, N., & Reynolds, P. (2010). Entrepreneurial behavior: Firm organizing processes. In Z. J. Acs & D. B. Audretsch (Eds.), *International handbook series on entrepreneurship* (Vol. 5, p. 121). New York, NY: Springer.

6 Nicolini, D. (2011). Practice as the site of knowing: Insights from the field of tele-medicine. *Organization Science, 22*(3), 602–620.

7 Mondada, L. (1998). Therapy interactions: Specific genre or "blown up" version of ordinary conversational practices? *Pragmatics, 8*(2), 155–166.

8 Baron, R. A., & Tang, J. (2009). Entrepreneurs' social skills and new venture performance: Mediating mechanisms and cultural generality. *Journal of Management, 35*(2), 282–306.

9 Lamine, W., Mian, S., & Fayolle, A. (2014). How do social skills enable nascent entrepreneurs to enact perseverance strategies in the face of challenges? A comparative case study of success and failure. International *Journal of Entrepreneurial Behavior and Research, 20*(6), 517–541.

10 Chalmers, D., & Shaw, E. (2017). The endogenous construction of entrepreneurial contexts: A practice-based perspective. *International Small Business Journal, 1*, 19–39.

11 Downing, S. (2005). The social construction of entrepreneurship: Narrative and dramatic processes in the coproduction of organizations and identities. *Entrepreneurship Theory and Practice, 29*(2), 185–204.

12 Fletcher, D. E. (2006). Entrepreneurial processes and the social construction of opportunity. *Entrepreneurship and Regional Development, 18*(5), 412–440.

13 Campbell, B. (2019). *Practice Theory in Action: Empirical Studies of Interaction in Innovation and Entrepreneurship*. New York, NY: Routledge.

APPENDIX

Toasted Marshmallow instructions and game materials

Toasted Marshmallow is a game to play with your teammates near the end of your shared work together. Most teams play it as they prepare to shut down a venture or just after they have done so. Others play it after they have negotiated an acquisition for their company. However, there is no wrong time to play it! As you know, there tend to be many ideas or product options that come to an end even while you continue to advance your venture.

Playing the *Toasted Marshmallow* game prompts conversations that can help your team process feelings, contextualize experiences, and reimagine next steps. The game uses question cards and post-game activity cards to stimulate conversations about the meaning(s) of the venture to each member of the team. In the following you will find the instructions for the *Toasted Marshmallow* game as well as two other clusters of materials; a set of basic question cards suitable for all players; an additional set of question cards for teams that are navigating an acquisition; a set of post-game challenge cards for teams that are failing forward; and a set of post-game challenge cards for teams that are navigating an acquisition.

And what is the origin of the game's name? Looking back on my own early ventures, I realized that those experiences had made me a "toasted marshmallow" – I was slightly burned by the experience but profoundly improved by it.

Instructions for playing the Toasted Marshmallow game

Setup

To play the *Toasted Marshmallow* game, the team copies and cuts out the appropriate sets of cards. The question cards are placed in a stack, question side down in the center of the table. The post-game challenge cards are placed in a separate stack, also question side down in the center of the table. Thirty-six "chips" (coins, paperclips, or other small tokens) are divided equally among the teammates. (If the chips do not divide equally, simply leave any excess chips to the side.)

Order of play

One team member draws a *Toasted Marshmallow* question card, reads the question aloud, and answers the question from his or her perspective. Going in a clockwise direction, other team members build on that first response by giving their own answer (which may sometimes contrast with the first teammate's perspective).

Any team member can give a chip to a player who has offered a very insightful or courageous answer. When you give a chip, you can elaborate on why you have decided to do so, or you can just give the chip without an explanation. When you receive a chip, you simply add it to your bank of chips.

There are no wrong answers, and a player can decline to answer any particular card. In instances when a player passes, other teammates should be given the chance to respond to the question card in the usual clockwise manner. After everyone has answered a question, your team can discuss the topic and reactions as briefly or extensively as you wish.

Players can continue to draw cards and respond in turn even if they have no remaining chips in their bank. The *Toasted Marshmallow* game ends when all the question cards have been used. The player with the most chips after the final question card has been drawn and answered by everyone wins.

The winner gets first pick from the deck of the *Toasted Marshmallow* post-game challenge cards (without looking at the content of the cards). Everyone picks a post-game challenge card and reads the challenge aloud. The players agree on an approximate timeline for enacting the challenges. Players go off to enact the challenges, and they reconnect, in-person or virtually, with the entire team at the later date to share the experience.

The game may take a minimum of 30 minutes to play. However, some teams have played the *Toasted Marshmallow* game for nearly 3 hours.

Toasted Marshmallow basic question cards for all teams

All teams should cut out and draw from these basic question cards. Additional question cards based on the current status of your venture can be found after this initial set of question cards.

Toasted Marshmallow
Question Card

If you could change
three things that you
did during the life of
the venture, what would
they be?

Toasted Marshmallow
Question Card

Think of your favorite
team moment during
the life of the venture.
What was it?

Toasted Marshmallow
Question Card

In what ways were you
unprepared to be an
entrepreneur at the start
of the venture?

Toasted Marshmallow
Question Card

What did success mean
to you at the start of the
venture? What does it
mean to you now?

Toasted Marshmallow
Question Card

What did you sacrifice
to try to do to make this
venture work? Would
you do that again? (If
not, what would you do
differently?)

Toasted Marshmallow
Question Card

Think back on the early
days of the venture:
How did we decide who
would do what? Would
we do something else
now?

Toasted Marshmallow
Question Card

What about the venture/
being an entrepreneur
worried you the most
as the venture was
just getting started?
Knowing what you know
now, were there more
important things to be
concerned about?

Toasted Marshmallow
Question Card

What was your most
embarrassing or
humbling moment
during the life of the
venture?

Toasted Marshmallow
Question Card

Think of the last
disagreement our
team had. How was it
resolved?

Toasted Marshmallow
Question Card

Who was your greatest
source of support during
the life of the venture?

Toasted Marshmallow
Question Card

Think of someone who
made a huge sacrifice to
try to make this venture
work. What did he or
she do, and why do you
think he or she did it?

Toasted Marshmallow
Question Card

What role has scarcity –
of time, money, trusted
relationships, food/
clothing/shelter, etc. –
played in making you
who you are?

Toasted Marshmallow
Question Card

Mark where you are on
this spectrum:

Start another venture
asap ↔ Never again

Toasted Marshmallow
Question Card

What do you admire
about the teammate
on your right based on
his or her role in and
contributions to the
venture?

Toasted Marshmallow
Question Card

If we made a movie
about our venture, what
genre would it be a
horror, comedy, drama,
adventure? Why?

Toasted Marshmallow
Question Card

What role has praise –
being praised or
expressing praise for
someone else – played in
your life?

Toasted Marshmallow
Question Card

Rank these descriptors in
terms of importance to
your identity:

entrepreneur, gender,
nationality, political party,
race, religion

Toasted Marshmallow
Question Card

Write a mission
statement for your life.
What is your purpose?
What is your life's
meaning?

Toasted Marshmallow
Question Card

Mark how worried you
were about personal
finances at the start of
the venture and how
worried you are about
them now.

Up all night worried ↔
Not worried at all

Toasted Marshmallow
Question Card

Think of a widely
admired person outside of
entrepreneurship (Martin
Luther King, Jr.; Abraham
Lincoln; etc.). What
advice do you imagine
that he or she would give
you at this point in your
life and career?

Toasted Marshmallow
Question Card

Why did you start this company?

To make money, to be my own boss, to have a big impact, something else?

Toasted Marshmallow
Question Card

What did we as a team do really well during the life of the venture?

Additional *Toasted Marshmallow* question cards for teams failing forward (FF)

Add these cards to the basic question card deck only if you are part of a team that is striving to fail forward.

Toasted Marshmallow
Question Card (FF)

The hardest thing about shutting down the venture was: telling my spouse/significant other/parents; dealing with vendors, customers, and other involved parties; coping with the financial aspects of the failure; other.

Toasted Marshmallow
Question Card (FF)

Which has suffered more by the failure of this venture?

Your professional reputation; your personal relationships; your bank account; other.

> *Toasted Marshmallow*
> **Question Card (FF)**
>
> Write a haiku eulogy for
> the venture.
> (A haiku is a three-
> line poem with a
> 5–7–5 syllabic structure.)

> *Toasted Marshmallow*
> **Question Card (FF)**
>
> If you had all the money
> in the world, what
> would you do next in
> your career?

Additional *Toasted Marshmallow* question cards for founding teams managing acquisitions (MA)

Add these cards to the basic question card deck only if you are part of a team that is managing an acquisition.

> *Toasted Marshmallow*
> **Question Card (MA)**
>
> The hardest thing about
> selling the venture was:
> letting go of "our baby";
> getting a new boss;
> telling my family; other.

> *Toasted Marshmallow*
> **Question Card (MA)**
>
> Write a haiku about the
> venture. (A haiku is a
> three-line poem with a
> 5–7–5 syllabic structure.)

Toasted Marshmallow
Question Card (MA)

What fears do you have
as we let go of this
venture and become
part of a new company?

Toasted Marshmallow
Question Card (MA)

The best thing about this
acquisition is . . . .

Toasted Marshmallow post-game challenge cards for teams failing forward (FF)

Use these cards for the post-game challenge only if you are part of a team that is striving to fail forward.

Toasted Marshmallow
Post-game Challenge (FF)

Think of your ideal
job. Find someone who
does that job and ask to
shadow them for a day.
After you've had that
experience tell your
teammates what it was
like.

Toasted Marshmallow
Post-game Challenge (FF)

Make a playlist of music
that could represent
the soundtrack for the
venture. Share it with
your teammates.

Toasted Marshmallow
Post-game Challenge (FF)

Think of a person who helped you a lot during the life of the venture. Write and send them an old-fashioned thank-you note.

Toasted Marshmallow
Post-game Challenge (FF)

Think of a kind of loss that is greater than a failed venture. Take a person who has experienced that difficulty to lunch and ask him or her about his or her recovery. Tell your teammates about any insights you've gained.

Toasted Marshmallow
Post-game Challenge (FF)

Write a short story from a perspective other than your own about the venture. Share it with your teammates.

Toasted Marshmallow
Post-game Challenge (FF)

Ask your teammates to craft a challenge just for you.

Toasted Marshmallow post-game challenge cards for founding teams managing an acquisition (MA)

Use these cards for the post-game challenge only if you are part of a team that is managing an acquisition.

Toasted Marshmallow
Post-game Challenge (MA)

Think of a person who helped you a lot during the life of this venture. Write and send them an old-fashioned thank-you note.

Toasted Marshmallow
Post-game Challenge (MA)

Make a playlist of music that could represent the soundtrack for the venture. Share it with your teammates.

Toasted Marshmallow
Post-game Challenge (MA)

Think of another entrepreneur whose company was acquired. Take him or her to lunch and ask about his or her post-venture transition. Tell your team about it.

Toasted Marshmallow
Post-game Challenge (MA)

Find an organization that helps first-time entrepreneurs in your area. Contact them and find out ways to give back. Tell your team about these opportunities.

Toasted Marshmallow
Post-game Challenge (MA)

Write a short story from
a perspective other than
your own about the
venture. Share it with
your teammates.

Toasted Marshmallow
Post-game Challenge (MA)

Ask your teammates to
craft a challenge just for
you.

GLOSSARY

Accelerator: An informal learning context for an aspiring entrepreneurial team. These spaces tend to focus on emerging ventures with the potential for rapid growth and strong financial returns. Many accelerators use a competition to select teams for each cohort. Selected teams tend to get physical space for working and guidance from advisors and/or investors. The cohorts usually assemble for a limited time (e.g., 3 or 4 months). At the conclusion of this time, advisors and investors affiliated with the accelerator may or may not opt to continue their involvement with any of the emerging ventures in the cohort.

Artifact: (see Documentation) The physical object created and captured by teammates engaged in the documentation process. An individual artifact can contribute to a specific pivot-or-persevere conversation; a set of artifacts captured over time can enable teams to understand and improve their habitual ways of working.

Brainstorming: A team activity that encourages the suggestion of ideas that are ungoverned by authentic aspects of the market, team, and other contextual features. It is distinct from provisional ways of knowing and interpreting which must remain anchored in aspects of the team's actual situation.

Collaborative language: Language forms that help teammates create productive interdependencies. It includes first-person plural pronouns (e.g., *we* and *ours*), heedfulness, and equal turn taking between team members in meetings.

Documentation: A process for team learning that includes phases of notation, discussion, and capture (of the artifact produced as a result of the documentation). It was developed for K–12 teachers and students at the Harvard University Graduate School of Education's Project Zero. In innovative entrepreneurial work, it is a means of making a team's interpretations visible and thereby available for analysis and discussion. It is especially useful in pivot-or-persevere meetings and other conversations associated with the major challenges of founding a venture.

Fail forward: The process of learning from a failed product or venture. The ability to generate new personal and professional identities based on the experience of a failure.

Innovative entrepreneurship: The work of entrepreneurial teams intent on creating new ventures based breakthrough products or services. It is distinct from imitative entrepreneurship which allows founders to open a venture within an established category (such as a new restaurant or dry cleaner).

Interpretive language forms: Verbal moves that promote innovation by supporting collaboration, provisional stances, and reflective dialogue.

Lean startup or Lean startup approach: A term and concept made popular by Eric Ries in a 2011 book by the same name; a method of new venture creation that relies on an iterative three-stage process of building a prototype, testing the prototype with prospective customers, and revising the prototype based on the results of the customer experiment.

Mindfulness: A term based on the research by Ellen Langer and advanced in her 1989 book by the same name; the act of noticing new things while maintaining an awareness of multiple perspectives. Contrasts with mindlessness.

Norms: (see Organizational culture)

Notation process: (see Documentation) An act of writing down core aspects of innovative entrepreneurial work; these notes are visible to the entire team as part of the documentation process.

Observational methods for innovating: Approaches to the development of new products and services that encourage the innovators to observe the experiences of the people who may use the new product or service. Examples include design thinking, human-centered design, and lean startup, among others.

Organizational culture: The assembly of materials, values, and assumptions that guide a team's routine work. The way a team talks creates, maintains, and evolves its organizational culture.

Pivot: A conscious change in direction based on evidence. The change can be relevant to the features of a product or service, the market segment, or the strategy of the organization.

Pivot-or-persevere meeting: A meeting in which an innovative entrepreneurial team reviews what they now know about their prototype, market, and resources such as time, money, and talent. The point of the meeting is to determine if the team should continue on the current trajectory or make a change to the emerging product or organizational strategy. The concept was made popular by *The Lean Startup* (Ries, E, 2011).

Provisional language: Language forms that help teams prevent premature cognitive commitments. It includes the use of conditional verbs (e.g., *could be, might*) and good-natured humor.

Reflective language: Language forms that allow teammates to reconsider their work. It includes opinion seeking, revisions to prior interpretations, and moves to suspend decision making. It is aided by mindfulness.

Retrospective meta-analysis: (See Documentation) An exercise that helps teams examine the assumptions and practices that characteristically shape their work. It requires a collection of captured artifacts from previous documentation processes. It may review subjects including consistencies repeated across meetings and toggling back and forth between one idea, an alternative idea, and back to the first idea.

Scaffolding for notation: (See Documentation) Preparations necessary to engage in the process of documentation. Includes the articulation of categories to guide the notation and discussion.

Situated humility or contextualized humility: A stance that allows an otherwise confident entrepreneur to accurately recognize and acknowledge his or her limitations in a particular situation.

Team: A small group of people who have a set of shared goals, possess the complementary skills necessary to meet those goals, and adhere to a set of norms while in pursuit of those goals.

INDEX

Note: Page numbers in *italics* indicate a figure and page numbers in **bold** indicate a table on the corresponding page.